Bell's Classical Arrangement of Fugitive Poetry

John Bell

Contents

EPISTLES..7
HEROIC AND AMATORY...7
EPISTLE I. 7
EPISTLE II. 17
EPISTLE III. 19
EPISTLE IV. 25
EPISTLE V. 29
EPISTLE VI. 40
EPISTLE VII. 54
EPISTLE VIII. 57
EPISTLE IX. 61
EPISTLE X. 65
EPISTLE XL. 71
EPISTLE XII. 79
EPISTLE XIII. 85
EPISTLE XIV. 96
EPISTLE XV. 102
EPISTLE XVI. 108
NOTES ON EPISTLES 122

HEROIC AND AMATORY..122
ELEGIES 138
ELEGY II. 141
ELEGY III. 144
ELEGY IV. 146
ELEGY V, ...150
ELEGY VI. 152
ELEGY VII. 153
ELEGY VIII. 157
ELEGY IX. 160
ELEGY X. 163
ELEGY XI. 172
ELEGY XII. 174
ELEGY XIII. 176
ELEGY XIV. 177
ELEGY XV. 180
ELEGY XVI. 183
ELEGY XVII. 187
ELEGY XVIII. 189
ELEGY XIX. 194
ELEGY XX. 198
ELEGY XXI. 211
ELEGY XXII. 213
ELEGY XXIII. 216
ELEGY XXIV. 220

ELEGY XXV.	224
ELEGY XXVI.	228
ELEGY XXVII.	231
ELEGY XXVIII.	235
ELEGY XXIX.	239
ELEGY XXX.	243
ELEGY XXX.	247
ELEGY XXXII.	251
ELEGY XXXIII.	252
ELEGY XXXIV.	254
ELEGY XXXV.	259
NOTES	267

BELL'S CLASSICAL ARRANGEMENT OF FUGITIVE POETRY

BY

John Bell

EPISTLES

HEROIC AND AMATORY.

EPISTLE I.

ROSAMOND TO KING HENRY.

BY WILLIAM PATTISON.

Qualis populea moereen Philomela tub umbra
Flet noétem, ramoque sedens miserabile carmen
Integral, et moestis late loca questions implet.

FROM these lone shades and ever-gloomy bowers,
Once the dear scenes of Henry's softer hours!
What tender strains of passion can impart
The pangs of absence to an amorous heart!
Far, far too faint the powers of language prove,
Language that slow interpreter of love!
Souls pair'd like ours, like ours to union wrought,
Converse by silent sympathy of thought;
0 then, by that mysterious art, divine

The wild impatience of my breast by thine ! .
And, to conceive what I would say to thee,
Conceive, my Love, what thou wouldst say to met
As in the tenderness of soul I sigh,
Methinks I hear thy tender soul reply ;
And as in thought, o'er heaps of heroes slain,
I trace thy progress on the fatal plain,
Perhaps thy thought explores me thro' the grove,
And, softening, steals an interval of love;
In the deep covert of a bowering shade
Describes my posture—languishingly laid!
Now, sadly solac'd with the murmuring springs,
Now, melting into tears, the softest things!
And how the feign'd ideas all agree!
So bowers the shade, so melt my tears for thee !
Here, as in Eden, once we blissful lay,
How oft night stole, unheeded, on the day !
Oar soft-breath'd raptures charm'd the listening grove,
And all was harmony, for all was love !
But hark ! the trumpet sounds ! see discords rise !
'Tis honor calls; from me my Henry flies!
Honor to him, more bright than Rosamonda's eyes!
Not thus my honor with his passion strove,
His sighs I pitied, and indulg'd his love:
He then cried, " honor was an empty name,
"And love a sweeter recompense than fiuae,

Oh I had I liv'd in some obscure retreat,
Securely fair, and innocently sweet;
How had I bless'd some humble shepherd's arms !
How kept-my fame as spotless as my charms!
idst thou ne'er beheld these eyes of mine
y bewail'd the fatal1 power of thine!

al power! to me for ever dear——
my tender breast, and rooted there !
- in my tender breast remain
for ever a delightful pain !

what surprize those glories first I view'd,
one moment my whole heart subdued !
ch resistless beams, so fierce they shone,
I the dazzling radiance of thy crown !
m thy crown ! never felt a dart;
er, not the monarch, won my heart:
the monarch with such charms appears,
the lover's soften'd dress he wears:
I he, silent, deigns my breast to seek,
ks such language as no tongue can speak.

he'er my crimes (if love a crime can be,
crime to live, and die for thee !)
tis forms arise, and cloud my soul,
Through of Henry can that gloom control:
my breast alternate passions move,
sts of honor melt before the fires of love.
I must repeat that fatal hour,
snatch'd my Henry from his Woodstock bower;
nad Bellona, with tumultuous cries,
o rouz'd, and drown'd the lover's sighs, .

Stretch'd on my downy couch at ease I lay,
And sought by reading to beguile the day;
With amorous strains I sooth'd a grateful fire,
And all the woman glow'd with soft desire.
'Till, as I wish'd, I heard the vocal breeze
Proclaim my Henry rustling thro' the trees

O'erjoy'd, I ran to meet thy longing arms,
And taste a dear remembrance of thy charms;
But soon I saw some sad concealed surprize,
Fade on thy cheeks, and languish on thine eyes ;
Thro' each dissembled smile a sorrow stole, .
And whisper'd out the secret of thy soul.
What this could mean uncertain to divine;
No fault I knew, yet fear'd some fault was mine.
But soon thy love dispell'd those airy fears,
Dispelled alas!—but brought too solid cares.
For as with hands, entwin'd in hands, we walk'd,
Of love, and hapless lovers, still thou talk'd:
Thy tears of pity answer'd each sad moan,
And in their seeming miseries wept thy own.
" I cannot leave her!"—I o'erheard thee say,—
Pierc'd to the soul, I sunk, and died away.
What art restor'd me, thou alone canst tell,
For thy kind arms embrac'd me as I fell.
My opening eyes fix'd on thy beauties hung,
And my ears drank the cordial of thy tongue.
Again my thoughts return with killing pain,
Within thy arms I sink, and swoon again:
Again thou dost my sweet physician prove,
From death to life alternately I move,
low dead by anguish, now reviv'd by love.
But when, without disguise, the truth I found,
My agonizing sorrows knew no bound:
My locks I tore; then all-intranc'd I lay,
Till by degrees my grief to words gave way,
And soft I cried,—" oh 1 stay, my Henry stay.
One moment more !—add yet,—and yet, a kiss!—
Oh! give me thine, and take my soul in this !
Farewell!—perhaps, farewell for ever!—oh !

Who can sustain so dire a weight of woe

Ah ! wretched Maid !—alas 1 a maid no more !
No herbs that spotless title can restore !
Ah! who shall now protect thy injur'd fame ?
Who shield thy weakness from th' assaults of shame ?
Who lull thy anxious soul to balmy rest,
If Henry, dearest Henry, flie thy breast ?

Yet, tho' he flie, your wings, ye Angels, spread,
And hover guardians o'er my Henry's head!
Who knows, but this kind prayer is pour'd too late,
And he already struggles with his fate ?
Already wounded, pants, and gasps in death,
And Rosamonda is his latest breath ?
Propitious Heaven! vouchsafe a gracious ear !
Grant these be only phantoms of my fear:
Heaven still is gracious, if true suppliants pray!
And lo !—-the foul chimeras fleet away !
Transporting prospects to my wishes rise,
Beam on my soul, ant! brighten in my eyes !
He lives! he lives ! I see his banner spread,
And laurels wreath'd round the gay victor's head!"
Ye winds! convey the news to Albion's floods !
Ye floods! resound it to the joyous woods!
Ye joyous woods! your tuneful choirs prepare
To hail my Hero from the toils of war!

Delusive scenes! too beautiful to stay!
They fade in visionary streaks away.
Alas! no lovely Henry now is nigh!
His Genius took his form to sooth my eye.
No more I seem his melting voice to hear !

Peace! babbling fountains 1 nor abuse my ear.
Ye flowers! ye streams! ye gales, no longer move!
For ah! how strong is fancy join'd with love!

O! frail inconstancy of mortal state!
One hour dejected, and the next elate !
Rais'd by false hopes, or by false fears deprest
How different passions sway the human breast !
Now smiling pleasures with fair charms invite,
Now frowning horrors with black trains affright.
Future distrusts the present joys control,
And fancy triumphs o'er the reasoning soul.

As mid the trees I solitary rove,
The trees awake some image of my love:
their arms in amorous foldings join,
arms I spread to fold in thine.
Ous flowers thy face reflected bear,
n beauty may with thee compare) .
d fragrancies thy breath inspire,
il kindles with ideal fire !
weav'd shades, and grove incircling grove,
ns of th' eternity of love,
g guilt the crimson roses paint,
roses, unsupported faint:
my youthful charms (if charms) consume,
closer canker, eats my bloom.

 might other Nymphs survey these scenes,
and shades, and hills, and flowery greens ?
i prospects might detain the sight,
triety give new delight.
thee, should find in deserts ease;

ee, not even Paradise could please:
hy presence, gardens would appear;
wild, since Henry is not here.
sink, or porticos arise,
view them with unpleasur'd eyes :
ling umbrage cools the noon-day fire,
in cool a lover's fierce desire ?

ep bosom of a darksome shade,
rew and mournful cypress made,
irtle weeps her ravish'd love,
irfully solaces the grove;
Sometimes my passion I aloud disclose;
The widow'd turtle, answering, cooes her woes.

Bred by my hand, my sorrow's sad relief,
A little linnet learns to sigh my grief;
Taught by my voice, and by obedience tame
The pretty lisper whistles Henry's name:
Perch'd on my head the sylvan syren sings,
And tunes the harsher notes of gurgling springs.

Embosom'd in a vale, thou know'st the shade,
Fast by the murmurs of a soft cascade:
There, while one night full beams of Cynthia play,
(Warm was the night) with wanderings tir'd, I lay,
Till, by degrees, the falling waters clos'd
My eye-lids, and my wearied limbs repos'd.
Sudden the fairy Monarch I behold,
Near he approaeh'd, and thus my fate foretold:
('Twas the same Oberon, that once we saw
Circle the-green, and give his dancers law.)

" Unhappy Nymph! thy beauty is thy crime—
And must such beauty perish in its prime!
No more great Henry shall enjoy those charms,
Nor thou ill-fated Fair adorn his arms!
Cropt like an opening rose, thy fall I fear!
But rise and supplicate the vengeance near.'
Then (as methought) I wak'd with threaten'd woes,
Emerging from thick shades a Phantom rose:

One hand sustained a short, but naked sword,—
I And one a golden bowl with poison stor'd:
The jealous Queen the frowning form express'd,
It spoke, and aim'd the dagger at my breast.

'Arise! nor ask thy crime—but choose thy fate,
Know prayers are vain—repentance is too late!
Vengeance is mine—Here! drink this poison'-d bowl,
Or this keen dagger drinks thy guilty soul!"
It ceas'd: convulsions in my bosom strove,
My curdling blood scarce in stiff tides could move.
Thrice I cried, " Henry!" with a feeble sound,
And thrice I started at the sad rebound!
Even echo now grew frightful: with surprize
Trembling I lay, nor dar'd unveil my eyes,
Till warbling birds proclaim'd the morning light,
And told me, 'twas a vision of the night;
Yet not the morn could chase my gloomy care,
But winds and trees alarm'd my soul with fear;
While waving boughs, that in the sun-beams play'd,
Seem'd to show daggers in each pointed shade.

Why was I form'd with such a coward mind?
The sport of shadows, or a rustling wind!

Nerves, better strung, did manly spirits warm,
Glad would I part with every female charm,
Then, cas'd in steel, the front of battle dare,
And, with great Henry, rouze the soul of war!
This arm should guard the Hero from the foe,
Repel the storm, or intercept the blow;
And should my weakness in the warrior fail
The soft-beseeching woman should prevail;
For thee I'd sooth each proud insulting foe,
And melt him with petitionary woe;
With thee in every hardy hazard join,
In danger save thy life to make it mine;
By night compose thy harrass'd head to rest,
And hush it on the pillow of my breast;
With patient eyes eternal vigils keep,
And court good Angels to protect thy sleep.

Alas! in vain I urge my frustrate will,
I find myself a feeble woman still;
The feeble woman to my breast returns,
For Henry's gone, and Rosamonda mourns !
O! see ray eyes their streaming anguish pour,
O! hear my sighs increase the swelling shower;
What can I more than shed my tears and sighs
Poor woman's strength alone in weakness lies.

But whither is ungovern'd fancy flown ?
Thoughts of impossibilities be gone!
Guilt claims no miracles, nor Heaven conspires.
To aid my crimes, and fan my lawless fires.
Life irksome grows; detested is the light,
And my soul dreads the visions of the night.
Swift let me to some hallow'd convent go !

Can I, for ever, Henry leave ?—ah ! no
But O lost Innocence !—I lost a name t—
O Honor!—broken is the bubble, fame.
Annoy sins monstrous ? do invented crimes,
Alike unknown to past or present times,
Demand red vengeance ? some peculiar curse ?
Crowds stand recorded for the same,—or worse.

' Have I, unpitying, heard the poor complain,
Or seen the wretched weep, and weep in vain?
Have I my flame feign'd for a sordid end ?
E'er wrong'd a foe, or e'er betray'd a friend ?
Not to my charge such crimes has malice brought,
Love, only love, is my unbounded fault s
A fault, that sure may Heaven to pity move,
Sineo-half of Heaven ('tis said) consists in love.

Ah! foolish Nymph!—Here, view the Queen! the laws!—
But there view Henry as th' enchanting cause !
By such a cause the priestess would retire,
And quit the vestal for a nobler fire.

I will again th' immortal Powers implore;
Brave Henry for Britannia's sake restore!
In him she lives, to him her joys are due,
And only sends her earliest thanks to you.
But O! my Lord, my darling Lord, beware!
Tempt not too bold the dangers of the war!
Think, when thou seest the fate-impelling dart,
O! think it aim'd at Rosamonda's heart!
Were but each breast as soft as mine, no more
Should tumults rise, or martial thunders roar:
Heroes should scorn the glories of the field,

And the fam'd laurel to the myrtle yield:
For sweeter passions sweeter strifes inspire,
And love alone should set the soul on fire.

May then these eyes in tears no longer mourn,
But cheerful hail their Henry's wish'd return !
O! swift, victorious, hush the war's alarms !
Swift, if thy Rosamonda boasts some charms,
Fly on the wings of Love and Conquest to her arms !

EPISTLE II.

KING HENRY
TO
ROSAMOND.
By the Same.

SHALL then his beauteous Rosamonda mourn,
Nor Henry's soul the soft complaint return ?
O cease, my Fair t I deeply feel thy smart,
And all thy sorrows double in my heart:
Far from my breast, ye scenes of war ! remove,
Far from my breast be every scene but love;
Soft rising thoughts as when, in Woodstock-bowers,
Joyful, we lov'd away the laughing hours.
Now midnight rest relieves the soldier's care,
Hush'd are the drums, and every voice of war;
Faint gleam the fires along the dewy field,
And faint the noise that sleeping coursers yield;
Yet Love, the lordly tyrant of my breast,
Alarms my soul, and interrupts my rest:
In vain a nation's cares the monarch move,
For ah ! far greater is the monarch Love!

Warm from my lips thy tender letter lies,
And every word is magic to my eyes;
Weeping, I read, and hear thy soft-breath'd woes,
And all the warrior in the lover lose:
Then I by fancy vanished joys restore,
Feast on false love, and act past pleasures o'er;
Fancy can sooth my soul with pleasing dreams,
While tented Gallia bowery Woodstock seems ;
Led by delusive steps, in thought I rove
Thro' well known greens, and every winding grove ;
There, haply on some flowery bank reclin'd,
My sweet-reposing Rosa mon da find;
When thou (for then thy secret thoughts I see)
In pious slumbers breath'st thy soul to me;
Dissolv'd with joy, and feasting on thy charms,
I clasp thee in imaginary arms;
And then—ah then!—- I seem sincerely blest—
Then only Rosamonda knows the rest—

O glories ! empires ! crowns! how weak ye prove,
If thus out-rivall'd by a dream of love!
O Love ! what joys thy real sweets bestow,
When even their shadows can transport me so!
O bliss extatic! blest relief from cares !
st me lose my soul in softer wars
transporting sighs my sweet alarms,
rlds, but Rosamonda crown my arms !
alone my full desires agree,
arms are empires, glories, all to me!

EPISTLE III.

FROM
DELAPOLE,
Duke of 8uffolk.
TO
MARGARET
Queen of Henry the Sixth.

BY W F.

OH royal Margaret, from the Kentish strand
Receive these tokens of thy Suffolk's hand,
And may kind Love the sacred change convey,
And love-born Zephyrs waft it on its way
To thee, thou pride, thou pleasure of my life,
Thou more than friend, than sister, or than wife t

At this sad hour, left friendless and alone,
With my lost greatness all my friends are flown.
Ah, fickle greatness! and ah, friends unkind !
Faith, friendship, duty, vanish into wiad!
Say, will my pen prove faithful to my woes,
And the sad story of my grief disclose,
This last sad scene of all my sorrows tell,
And bid the darling of my soul farewell ?

>ass'd the dread decree which bade me roam,
ng years, an exile from my home;
 Oppression sanctify'd by Might,

ne, hallow'd by the name of Right,
I with impious hand my fair domains,
i forests, and paternal plains;
keen Malice, watchful to destroy,
proud domes, once fill'd with mirth and
oy; urimov'd the dreadful tale I hear,
the mighty ruin worth a tear.
ny life! I shed for thee alone
cnt tear, and heav'd the ceaseless groan.
nt to my soul, in act to part, idea clung
around my heart; not there thy image been
enshrin'd, t had danc'd all lightly as the wind:
I with scorn, I then had left the land,
ed pleasure on another strand.
ly sex ! believe me, whilst I swear
t alone the cause of all my care;
all my former feats of arms,
i oath more sacred, by thy charms.

i exile, (such the stern decree!)
ng years from happiness and thee;
le night in woe, and waste away,
lplaints and vain, the lengthening day:
stranger in a friendless land
tits the tedious hours with sparing hand.

Now whilst his lot each wretched captive mourns,
To Kent's dread shore the bounding bark returns.
Flush'd with success, each nerve the robbers strain,
Hoist the broad sail, and measure back the main;
And soon we view, for well they plied their pars,
The rising mountains, and approaching shores,
Th' approaching shores we view with anxious eye,

Drop the vain tear, and heave the fruitless sigh.

Whilst in dumb sorrow on the deck I lay,
And casta long glance o'er the watery way,
Th' unfeeling leader wounds my anguish'd ear –
With many a foul reproach and many a sneer,
Arraigns my warlike deeds, insults my name,
Nor'spares th' unfeeling wretch my Margaret's fame;
Then, pointing to the strand, henries, "
'Tis nigh, That is thy dcstin'dport, prepare to die !"

I heard unmov'd, and now th' increasing gales.
Propitious blew, and fill'd the swelling sails,
Near and more near we draw, we gain the strand,
And the sharp keel divides the yellow sand.

A cliff there is, which rears its rocky steep
In awful state, and trembles o'er the deep,
Scarce can the wanderer on the beach below

Lift his tir'd eye to gain the mountain's brow,
For oft from mortal view thick vapors shroud
Its misty top, and wrap it in a cloud;
What time with rising ray the Lord of light
Io Eastern climes exalts his banners bright,
Or when, more mild, in purple tints array'd,
Forth from the West he casts a lengthening shade.

Here must I fall, fast by the rolling main
(Nor was the mutter'd spell pronounc'd in vain,
When rose th' infernal Spirit, whilst by night
The sorceress plied th' unutterable rite),
Here bid adieu to crowns, to cares, and strife,

To Margaret and to joy, to love, and life.

But ere my body, on the cold beach spread,
Is mangled thrown, and number'd with the dead,
Let me, to sooth my sorrows, let me cast

One parting view on all my pleasures past,
Nor will my fate deny this transient stay,
Nor will my Margaret blame the lengthened lay.

In youthful bloom I plac'd my sole delight
In warlike exercise and feats of fight;
And, more mature, I left the listed plain,
And sought renown in tented fields to gain;
But when to Tours, thy residence,
I came, Unnumber'd beauties fann'd my rising flame;
I gaz'd in speechless rapture on thy charms,
Forgot the tented plain, the feats of arms,
Forgot the listed field, the marshal'd host,
And all the warrior in the lover lost.

Thus I, who 'scap'd the sword and javelin's power,
Launch'd by the foe in danger's darkest hour,
Who 'scap'd th' embattled war and ambush'd fight,
Who 'scap'd dire force by day, and fraud by night,
Undaunted by the woes that wait on arms,
Fall, vanquish'd fall, the victim of thy charms.

Oh vale of Tours, and Loire, maeandering flood,
On whose green bank my Margaret first I view'd;
Oh lovely stream! and oh enchanting grove!
How often have ye heard my tale of love!
Maeandering Loire ! how often hast thou seen

This faded form upon thy banks of green,
Seen me with folded arms and visage pale,
Seen my despair, and heard my hapless tale!
And she, the nymph that holds her airy reign '
Mid the steep rocks that tremble o'er the plain,
Lone Echo, musing maid, was wont to stray
Where'er I went, the partner of my way;
Whether I wander'd by the neighboring tide,
Or vent'rous climb'd the mountain's cultur'd sid:
Or whether choice my wandering steps invite,
To where, unenvious of the mountain's height,
Of lordships wide and princely treasures vain,
The Benedictine rears his stately fane:
Aloft in air the gorgeous mansion springs,
And towers disdainful of the pomp of kings:
Where'er I wander'd, still the nymph was nigh,
Answer'd my griefs, and gave me sigh for sigh.
what delight, amid the landscape gay,
ow stream winds his pleasurable way,
iuch delight my life's smooth current
roll'd, allow'd my Margaret to behold,
ih ! so sad, so languid, and so slow,
doom'd by Fate thy presence to forego !
in mute wonder on thy face I gaze,
3ubts distract, alarm me, and amaze; .,
I pause, and many a scheme revolve,
the last I fix'd my firm resolve;
ras my plan proposed, and soon approv'd,
1 for Henry, for myself I lov'd,
ive, in change for thee, thy Sire to reign
rtile Anjou, and the fields of Maine.
traight, for love like mine ill brook'd delay,
gland's court I bent my hasty way,

on the tale to Henry's ear convey'd,
soft persuasion gave me all her aid; rd the
soft told tale with favoring ear,
ajh'd in secret for the pictur'd fair:
'd the gradual growth of young desire,
ded fuel to the rising fire;
It now alone remains to waft her o'er
From Gallia's coast to England's happier shore.

I spoke. Th' attendant lords, with zealous care,
And costly art my princely train prepare;
Soon in her port my gallant vessel rode,
And soon receiv'd with joy her precious load.
And soon my beauteous Queen was wafted o'er
From Gallia's coast to England's happier shore.

When bright in all her charms my Margaret came,
Faction was hush'd, and Pride forgot to blame,
Thy beauty was the theme of every tongue,
Was prais'd By grave and gay, by old and young ;
That winning air, that heavenly smile, disarms
E'en Envy's self, enamor'd of thy charms;
She dwells in rapture on thy faultless face,
Majestic mien, and more than mortal grace.

How did thy charms thy Suffolk's bosom move!
How deeply did he drink the draught of Love!
For not the crown that bound thy beauteous brow
Woke my warm wish, or drew the venal vow:
I scorn'd the pageant toys, for, bless'd with thee,
Ah, what were sceptres, what were crowns to me
Nor gorgeous crowns, nor regal sceptres move;
I listen'd only to the voice of Love.

or ah! the ruthless ruffian chides my stay,
And envious Death denies this short delay;
enies me longer on the theme to dwell :
More lov'd than life, my beauteous Queen, farewell !

EPISTLE IV.

FROM
MARY
Queen of France, TO
CHARLES BRANDON
Duke of Suffolk..

LET these soft lines my kindest thoughts convey,
And tell thee what I suffer by thy stay.
Did seas divide us, this might well excuse
Thy negligence, and my fond heart abuse.
But Calais from the Kentish strand is seen;
A gentle current only rolls between.
Nor needs my Suffolk, like Leander, brave
A present death in every breaking wave,
When, guided only by a glimmering light,
He crooss'd the stormy Hellespont by night.
Tall ships, with flying sails and laboring oars,
Attend to land thee on the Gallic shores.

But thou art chang'd—that ardor is expir'd,
Which once thy wishes with impatience fir'd ;
When Savoy's blooming duchess strove in vain
From me the conquest of thy heart to gain ;
loble torm th unguarded fair surpnz'd;
^ere her tender wishes long disguis'd : ever

Flattery, Love, or wanton Art,
I do, she practis'd to seduce thy heart.
Antony, by such allurements gain'd, leopatra all
his glory stain'd: ly firm faith no injury received;
ou still lov'd, or I was well deceiv'd:
jere my virgin vows less true to thee, i young
Castile address'd the court for me. :
harms of proffer'd empire I resign'd;
Ion was more than empire to my mind:
without rivals, in thy breast I reign'd,
loughts the pageantry of power disdain'd.
ah I what changes human joys attend!
Jde turns our brightest hopes depend, rious
Henry's arms still meet sugcess; ranquish'd
Gauls at last propose a peace.

But Love entirely had my soul possess'd.
How oft I wish'd my kinder destiny
Had sunk the Queen in some obscure degree;
While, crown'd by rural maids with painted flowers
I rang'd the fields, and slept in verdant bowers;
Belov'd of some young swain, with Brandon's face,
His voice, his gesture, and his blooming grace,
In all but birth and state resembling thee !
Then unmolested we had liv'd, and free
From all the curst restraints which greatness brings;
While grots, the meads, the shades, and purling springs,
The flowery valley, and the gloomy grove,
Had heard of no superior name to Love.
Such scenes of this inglorious life I drew,
And half believ'd the charming fiction true,
Till real ills dissolv'd the pleasing dreams,
The groves and vallies fled, the lawns and silver streams.

The gay fantastic paradise I mourn'd;
While courts and factions, crowns and cares, return'd.

With sighs I still recall the fatal day,
When no pretence could gain a longer stay.
The lovely Queen my parting sorrow saw,
Nor Henry's presence kept my grief in awe.
No rules of decent custom could control,
Or hide the wide disorder of my soul,
When shipp'd for France before the dancing wind
The navy fled and left my hopes behind.
With weeping eyes I still survey'd the strand,
Where on a rising cliff I saw thee stand ;
Nor once from thence my stedfast sight withdrew,
Till the lov'd object was no more in view.
" Farewell, I cry'd, dear charming Youth! with thee
Each chearful prospecl vanishes from me."

Loud shouts and triumphs on the Gallic coast
Salute me; but the noisy zeal was lost.
Nor shouts nor triumphs drew my least regard,
Thy parting sighs, methought, were all I heard.
But now at Albeville by Louis met,
I strove the thoughts of Suffolk to forget;
For here my faith was to my monarch vow'd,
And solemn rites my passion disallow'd:
However pure my former flames had been,
Unblemish'd honor made them now a sin.
But scarce my virtue had the conquest gain'd,
And every wild forbidden wish restraint ;
When at St. Dennis, with imperial state
Invested, on the Gallic throne I sate;
The day with noble tournaments was grac'd,

Your name amongst the British champions plac'd.
Invited by a guilty thirst of fame,
Without regard to my repose, you came.
The lists I saw thee entering with surprize,
And felt the darting glances of thine eyes.

" Ye sacred Powers, I cry'd, that rule above!
Defend my breast from this perfidious love !
Ye holy Lamps? before whose aweful lights
I gave my hand; and ye religious rites !
Assist me now; nor let a thought unchaste,
Or guilty wish, my plighted honor blast Pi-
While passion, struggling with my pious fears,
Forc'd from my eyes involuntary tears,
Some tender blossom thus, with leaves enlarg'd,
Declines its head, with midnight dew o'ercharg'd:
The passing breezes shake the gentle flowex,
And scatter all around a pearly shower.
From this distracting hour I shunn'd thy sight,
And gain'd the conquest by a prudent flight.
But human turns, and sovereign destiny,
Have set me now from those engagements free.
The stars, propitious to my virgin love,
My first desires and early vows approve;
While busy politicians urge in vain,
That public reasons should my choice restrain;
That none but York's or Lancaster's high race.
Or great Plantagenet's, I ought to grace!
Nor Suffolk wants a long illustrious line,
And worth that shall in future records shine.
They own'd thy valor when thy conquering lance
Carry'd the prize from all the youth of France.
Thy merit Henry's constant favor shows,

And Envy only can my choice oppose.
Thy noble presence, wit, and fine address,
The British and the Gallic court confess.
Alancon's shape, and Vendöme's sparkling eye,
Count Paul's gay mien, and Bourbon's majesty,
jer are admir'd, when thou art by.
nothing wants to justify my flame,
tesmen grant, but a poor empty name. hat's
the gaudy title of a King ?
olid bliss can royal grandeur bring ? :
hou art absent, what's the court to me,
:some state, and dull formality ? y a crown
I would resign, to prove
aceful joys of innocence and love.

EPISTLE V.

FROM
LADY JANE GRAY
TO
LORD GUILFORD DUDLEY.

SUPPOSED TO HAVE BEEN WRITTEN IN THE TOWBR,
A FEW DAYS BEFORE THEY SUFFERED.

BY 6. KEATE, ESQ.

Quis Regni posrhac confidet viribus? aut quern
Gloria decipiet Sceptri, Soliive superbi
Lubrica Majestas ? Supplem. Lucan.

FROM these dread walls, this melancholy Tow'r,
Doom'd the sad victim of relentless Pow'x,
Where Ruin sits in gloomy pomp array'd,

And circling horrors spread their mournful shade,.
I send the tribute of a short'ning life,
The last memorial of a faithful Wife.
For ev'ry hope on this side Heav'nis fled,
And Death's pale banner waves around my head.
It yet perchance may cheer my Lord to know
That SUFFOLK'S Daughter sinks not with her woe:
spite of all, one anxious thought survives,
lee, my GUILFORD, 'tis for Thee it lives.
hou alone with Heav'n divid'st my heart,
11 Heaven's due, yet Nature gives Thee part.
be still a crime, I'm guilty still,
forget, depends not on our will.
on once deep rooted in the breast,
etimes shook, tho' rarely dispossest;
ding passion there in triumph reigns,
is my weakness, but augments my pains.
le dear past my roving fancy flies,
rings thy image to my raptur'd eyes.
urner's weeds, no captive's chain it wears,
ight in all its native charms appears;
race, such virtue beaming from thy brows,
le my heart, and fix'd my virgin vows;
is Thou wert, when at the altar's side
But from Man's weakness still some comfort flows,
'Tis that he nought beyond the present knows ;
Heav'n draws a friendly curtain o'er his doom,
And hides in deepest shades each ill to come-
Then be its will ador'd, which, understood,
From seeming mischief draws forth certain good.
Nor in these lines suspect that I complain,
Tho' mem'ry loves to trace past time again.

Thus do I waste the solitary day,
With tedious pace thus creep my hours away;
And when the Moon, rob'd in her paler light,
Revisits mortals, and direös the Night,
If then my weary'd strength some slumber shares,
The Soul reflecting wakes to ail her cares;
Delusion o'er my mind usurps command,
And rules each sense with Fancy's magic wand.
One moment tidings of forgiveness brings,
Descending Mercy speads her cherub wings;
Our guards are vanish'd, ev'ry grief effae'd,
We meet again, embracing and embrae'd.—
O bliss supreme! but too supreme to last;
Ere words can find their way, the vision's past:
It fleets, I call it back—it will not hear,
And fearful shadows in its place appear.
The unrelenting Queen stalks fiercely by,
Fate on her brow, and fury in her eye.
Hark! the dread signal that compleats our woes :
Hark! the loud shoutings of our barb'rous Foes!
I see the axe rear'd high above thy head,
It-falls!—and GUILFORD'S numbered with the dead.
Alas ! how ghastly !——Ev'ry vein streams blood,
And the pale corpse sinks in the crimson flood.
Could that sad Form be once my Soul's delight?—
Quick tear the mad'ning Phantom from my sight.
Hold, hold your hands, ye Ministers of Fate,
Suspend the blow, lest Mercy come too late;
Let Innocence at last your pity move,
And spare my Lord, my Husband, and my Love!—
NORTHUMBERLAND ! Thee, Thee could I upbraid,
And bid Thee view the ruin thou hast made.
This tragic picture thy ambition plann'd,

And all its colors own thy daring hand.
But thou art fall'n !—Nor shall my parting breath
Call out for vengeance in the hour of death:
I as thou wert, am to the Scaffold doom'd,
Soon with my ancestors must lie entomb'd;
With the wofld's transient contests I have done,...
The hastening sands of life are nearly run ;
A moment such as this, is not the time
To blame thy weakness, or reproach thy crime!
May all remembrance of thy guilt subside,
And the dark grave thy dust and frailties hide !

The searching eye of Heav'n, whose wisdom darts
Thro' all the mean disguises of our hearts,
And ev'ry silent motive, knows alone
With what reluctance I approached the throne.
I never sigh'd for Grandeur's envy'd rays,
For regal Honors, or a Nation's praise.
My bosom never felt Ambition's fire;
For what exchange could GUILFORD'S Wife desire ?
The bloom of MAY beneath our feet was spread,
And all its roses deck'd our nuptial bed.
With Thee conjoin'd, each social joy I found;
With Thee conversing, Pleasure breath'd around.
To prize the world aright, and form the mind
To my lov'd books my leisure I resign'd:
Or absent thou, to cheer the ev'ning's gloom,
Encircled with my Maidens, ply'd the Loom.
PEACE was my Sister, and my Friend CONTENT,
The best companion e'er to mortals sent;
Plac'd at my side, they tun'd their soothing lyres,
And sung those carols Innocence inspires,
But when, obedient to a Father's pow'r,

And the last wish of EDWARD'S dying hour,
Destructive counsel t I my home forsook,
Assum'd the purple, and the sceptre took,
Swift from my sight the heav'nly Pair withdrew.
And Friend and Sister bade me both adieu.

Let such as, flatter'd by a pompous name,
Risk their own quiet in pursuit of Fame,
Beware th' exchange; awhile their purpose turn,
And from a ***wretched Queen*** one moral learn.
It is the cheat of ev'ry worldly joy,
To tempt when distant, but possess'd to cloy;
Hence flows a truth of much import, 'tis this;
" Content's the highest pitch of human bliss."
Strange we should then the proffer'd boon reject !
All know to seek it, yet the search neglect.
To no one soil, no station 'tis confin'd,
Springing, if cultur'd, in each steady mind,
Far from Ambition's fiery trait it flies,
But lives with Virtue, and with Virtue dies !

O had our lot by kinder stars been thrown
Beneath some lonely shade, to Fame unknown ;
Far from those scenes remov'd, where Pride resorts,
Far from the Cares, far from the Crimes of Courts,
Unconscious of the thorns which wound the Great,
Our lengthen'd years had own'd a happier fate :
Pleas'd with our fortune, by ourselves approv'd,
Secure from Envy, and by all belov'd.
Whilst, from a busy, faithless World retir'd,
By no blind folly vex'd, no passion fir'd,
Calmly we then afar had heard the strife,
The noise, the tumult that perplexes life;

Smil'd at Contention's visionary plan,
And the vain toils of self-deluded man.

Yet cease, my heart, these plaintive murmurs cease;
For why, my GUILFORD, should I wound thy peace ?
Why with imagin'd joys thy thoughts, engage,
Since we are fetter'd on a tragic stage ?
But say, what Tyranny can reach the Soul ?
What Terrors shake her, or what Force control ?
Immortal as the Pow'r from whence she springs,
Sick of her home, she mounts on Fancy's wings,
With inborn Freedom nourish'd, spurns her chains,
And roves unbounded thro' ideal scenes !
Ideal joys are all I now have left,
Of Thee, a Crown, and Liberty bereft;
Torn from the pleasures of domestic life,
From each fond rapture of a virtuous Wife:
By all Hope here forsaken ! 'tis in vain
That Reason whispers I should not complain:
A sigh will heave, in spite of all my pow'rs ;
And sighs are due to miseries like ours.
Ha! meet no more ! How cruel the decree!—
Heart-rending sentence ! No It must not be.
Down prison walls, each obstacle remove,
And let me clasp once more the Man I love !
One parting look a wretched Wife desires;.
One parting kiss the seal of Death requires !
And is there none to plead th' Unhappy's suit ?
All ears are deaf, andev'ry tongue is mute!
Then, come the worst—Yet, howsoe'er distrest,
Still shall thy Image live within my breast;
My senses still that object shall pursue,
And each fond wish be offer'd up for You.

Tho', all unfeeling for this bleeding heart,
Our Foes dismiss to Heav'n thy nobler part,
Deep in the dust thy injur'd form I'll trace,
And grudge th' unconscious grave its cold embrace.
But hold thy hand, presumptuous Woman, hold;
Too warm thy passion, as thy pen too bold.
Far other thoughts the present hour demands,
Lo! at my side the shadowy Monarch stands;
Aid me, great Teacher, this hard conflict end,
Tho' **King of Terrors** call'd, I'll hail thee *Friend* !
Since thou alone portray'st to mortal eyes
How weak, how baseless are the joys we prize ff
Thou mock'st our useless toils, our mimic state,
And warn'st a brother, by a brother's fate!
Thy moral then shall not be lost on me,
Convinc'd, my Soul approves the just decree;
And unrepining quits this scene of strife,
Which points thro' Virtue to a happier Life.

The Priest this morn, with every art endu'd,
Th' accursed purpose hath again renew'd;
" Be ours," he cries, " our better faith embrace, "
And live preserver of your falling race. "
Tho' yet misled, stand forth the child of ROME,
" The Queen, in mercy, will avert your doom."
Merciful Queen ! Yet since thus greatly kind,
Tell us what mercy shall th' Apostate find ?
Thy royal mandate may decide our fates,
But Peace alone on conscious duty waits;
Who wars against it, does the work of hell,
And arms a Daemon he can never quell;
Whose shafts receiv'd, search the wide globe around,
Nor herb, nor balsam heals the fatal wound.

Bear back, false WINCHESTER, thy proffer'd bliss,
Weigh crowns and kingdoms with a deed like this,
Far, far too light in Wisdom's eye they seem,
Nor shake the scale, while Reason holds the beam.
And can she, GUILFORD, deem me sunk so low,
So fondly wedded to this world of woe,
To think her bounty would my fears entice
To purchase fleeting breath at such a price?
' Which when obtain'd, the poor precarious toy.
A thousand ills might weaken, or destroy?
No Since I'm sworn a sister to Mischance,
Let the clouds gather, let the storm advance,
Unmov'd, its bursting horrors I'll defy,
And steady to my faith a Martyr die.
For Life's, alas! too like the transient rose,
Which oft is blasted the same day it blows;
Its beauty from the wind a blight receives,
Orsome foul canker taints its crimson leaves
Nor judge it hard to fall an early flow'r,
Rescu'd perchance from some tempestuous shower,
From noxious vapors arm'd with force to kill,
The noontide sunbeam, or the ev'ning's chill.
Howe'er the thought appal, Death's gloomy road
By ev'ry mortal foot must once be trod!
Deep thro' the Vale of Tears man's journey lies,
And sorrow best prepares him for the skies 1
0 then, my Husband, I conjure thee, hear,
If SUFFOLK'S Daughter e'er to Thee was dear,
By ev'ry wish of happiness to come, —
By ev'ry hope beyond the mouldering tomb;
If anxious that thy better fame should soar,
And shine applauded when the Man's no more:
Let not the wily Churchman win thine ear,

Or sooth thy weakness by his fraudful care;
But arm'd with Constancy's unfailing shield,
As God's own soldier valiant, scorn to yield.
So when Religion, stript of each disguise,
In ancient purity again shall rise,
To her true throne once more shall be restor'd,
And rule by **Reason**, stronger than the **Sword**,
Posterity our merits may attest,
And our fair deeds by all good men be blest.
In distant times, then shall old people tell
How firmly GUILFORD and his Consort fell.
To all their list'ning family relate,
How our faith triumph'd, though our woes were great.
Then shall each youth and maid our names revere,
Grace our sad story with a gen'rous tear,
And give our dust this **Requiem** with a sigh,
" Peace guard the shrine where Virtue's Children lie."

O ,JHOU SUPREME, on whom we all depend,
Our common Parent, and our common Friend,
Who deign'st to watch us from thy distant skies,
Bidding the pray'rs of humbled suff'rers rise,
Ruler of Heaven, stretch forth thy mighty hand,
And save from civil rage my native land.
Let ROME'S ambitious sons no more prevail,
Blast all their hopes, and let their counsels fail.
Raise up some Prince to perfect that great plan
Thy servant EDWARD (under Thee) began;
That Error's clouds dispers'd, may ne'er return,
And thy pure light with fires rekindled burn.
So, Peace, sad fugitive, again shall smile,
And fix her dwelling on this prosper'd Isle.-

Whilst for myself one only boon I crave,
Support that fortitudethy Mercy gave;
The heart thou mad'st, preserve severely just
Firm in its fate, and steady to its trust.
There, whilst it beats, thy praise shall ever reign,
Live, whilst it lives, and flow in ev'ry vein :
Praise the sole tribute I have left to give,
Nay, ail a GOD from Mortals can receive.

Come then, my Lord, my Husband, and my Love
(For Death alone those titles shall remove)
With decent courage meet thy certain doom,
Nor shrink with horror at the op'ning tomb.
What from the grave can virtue have to fear?
'Tis peace, 'tis refuge from the worst despair;
All strife, all human contests 'twill adjust,
Nor can the hand of Pow'r insult the dust!
Religion sitting by the Mourner's side
Inspires that comfort which the World deny'd;
And, 'midst our woes, of this one truth we're sure,
Whate'er is mortal cannot long endure.
Our pains, as well as joys, soon find an end,
And, tir'd of both, we call our shroud a Friend!—
Meet it as such, my GUILFORD, nor thy soul
O'er-awe with fancy, or with fear control,
Think, 'twill the rigor of thy lot repay,
Think, 'tis a passport to the realms of day.
On Faith's strong pinions thou shalt wing thy flight,
And (the World conquer'd) with the Blest unite.
The pomp of Death, the scaffold, and the steel,
The Man recoiling, may an instant feel,
For Nature will be heard; but be thy mind
Warm with its future prospects, and resign'd

What then remains for me?—Ah! wherefore ask?—
Fain would my trembling pen avoid the task;
Here would it stop, nor wake thy suff'rings more,
But idle ceremony now is o'er;
These tear-stain'd lines must their whole purpose tell,
And bid my dying Lord a last farewell.
A last! a long farewell! Oh cruel sound,
It pains, it tears, it harrows up my wound.
Alas! the transient dream!—Down, rebel Heart,—
Yet, keen their pangs that must for ever part!
A thousand, thousand things I had to say,
But the fleet minutes suffer no delay.
Might these fond eyes once more that form behold
These arms, tho' 'twere in death, my Love enfold?
A Woman's weakness sure might be forgiven,
And this last frailty be absolv'd by Heav'n,
'Twas a rash wish;—no—shun me,—for I fear
A final interview we could not bear!
Ere yet a little space, this scene will close,
And end the malice of our ruthless foes.
Arm'd as we are for Fate, we'll die content;
Fortune hath done its worst, its rage is spent.
To happier mansions we shall soon remove,
And meet in bliss, for we shall meet above,
Crown'd with eternal peace, we then shall own
How poor the contest for a worldly throne!
No feuds, no treasons can our joys molest,
Or shake th' immortal triumphs of the Blest!
And see, our wish'd-for haven is not far,
This hope shall cheer us like a guiding star;
Safe in our sea-beat bark we'll stem the flood,
And spread each sail to meet the coming Good.—
Descend, my Guardian Angel, from the skies,

In my firm breast let dauntless Virtue rise;
Loose, loose all ties that hold me captive here,
And from my mem'ry blot what most was dear.
Yes, my Deliverer, yes, I find thy aid;
Each passion's calm, and all the storm is laid.
I felt its influence, GUILFORD, as I spoke ;
The complicated chain at length is broke ;
E's vain enchantments all have ta'en their flight,
d Earth diminish'd fades before my sight;
last, sad, parting sigh is left for You ;
rest is Heav'n's:—a long—long—long Adieu!

EPISTLE VI.

FROM
LORD WILLIAM RUSSEL
TO
WILLIAM LORD CAVENDISH.

BY GEO. CANNING, ESQ.

LOST to the world, to-morrow doom'd to die,
Still for my country's weal my heart beats high.
Tho' rattllng chains ring peals of horror round,]
While Night's black shades augment the savage sound,
Midst bolts and bars the active soul is free,
And flies, unfetter'd, CAVENDISH, to thee.

Thou dear companion of my better days,
When hand in hand we trod the paths of Praise;
When, leagu'd with patriots, we maintain'd the cause
Of true religion, liberty, and laws,
Disdaining down the golden stream to glide,

But bravely stemm'd Corruption's rapid tide;
Think not I come to bid thy tears to flow,
Or melt thy generous soul with tales of woe;
No: view me firm, unshaken, undismayed,
As when the welcome mandate I obey'd
Heavens! with what pride that moment I recall !
Who would not wish, so honor'd, thus to fall !
When England's Genius, hovering o'er, inspir'd
Her chosen sons, with love of Freedom fir'd,
Spite of an abject, servile, pensioned train,
Minions of Power, and worshippers of Gain,
To save from Bigotry its destin'd prey,
And shield three nations from tyrannic sway.

'Twas then my CA'NDISH caught the glorious flame,
The happy omen of his future fame;
Adorn'd by Nature, perfected by Art,
The clearest head, and warmest, noblest heart,
His words deep sinking in each captiv'd ear,
Had power to make even Liberty more dear.

While I, unskill'd in Oratory's lore,
Whose tongue ne'er speaks but when the heart runs o'er,
In plain blunt phrase my honest thoughts express'd
Warm from the heart, and to the heart address'd.
Justice 1prevail'd ; yes Justice, let me say,
Well pois'd her scales on that auspicious day.
The watchful shegherd spies the wolf afar
Nor trusts his flock to try the unequal war;
What tho' the savage crouch in humble guise,
And check the fire that flashes from his eyes,
Should once his barbarous fangs the fold invade,
Vain were their cries, too late the shepherd's aid,

Thirsting for blood, he knows not how to spare,
His jaws distend, his fiery eyeballs glare,
While ghastly Desolation, stalking round,
With mangled limbs bestrews the purple ground.

Now, Memory, fail 1 nor let my mind revolve,
How England's Peers annull'd the just resolve,
Against her bosom aim'd a deadly blow,
And laid at once her great Palladium low !

Degenerate nobles! Yes, by Heaven I swear,
Had BEDFORD'S self appear'd delinquent there,
And join'd, forgetful of his country's claims,
To thwart the exclusion of apostate JAMES,
All filial ties had then been left at large,
And I myself the first to urge the charge.

Such the fix'd sentiments that rule my soul,
Time cannot change, nor Tyranny control;
While free, they hung upon my pensive brow,
Then my chief care, my pride and glory now
Foil'd I submit, nor think the measure hard,
For conscious Virtue is its own reward.
Vain then is force, and vain each subtile art,
To wring retraction from my tortured heart;
There lie, in marks indelible engrav'd,
The means whereby my country must be sav'd;
Are to thine eyes those characters unknown ?
To read my inmost heart, consult thine own;
There wilt thou find this sacred truth reveal'd,
Which shall to-morrow with my blood be seal'd.
Seek not infirm expedients to explore,
But banish JAMES, or England is no more.

Friendship her tender offices may spare,
Nor strive to move the unforgiving pair,
Hopeless the tyrant's mercy-seat to climb
Zeal for my country's freedom is my crime !
Ere that meets pardon, lambs with wolves shall range,
CHARLES be a saint, and JAMES his nature change.

Press'd by my Friends, and RACHEL'S fond desires,
(Who can deny what weeping love requires!)
Frailty prevail'd, and for a moment quell'd
Th' indignant pride that in my bosom swell'd;
I sued—the weak attempt I blush to own
I sued for mercy, prostrate at the throne.
O! blot the foible out, my noble friend,
With human firmness human feelings blend!
When Love's endearments softest moments seize,
And Love's dear pledges hang upon the knees,
When Nature's strongest ties the soul enthrall,
Thou canst conceive, for thou hast felt them all!)
Let him resist their prevalence, who can;
He must, indeed, be more or less than man.

Yet let me yield my RACHEL honor due,
The tenderest wife, the noblest heroine too !
Anxious to save her husband's honest name,
Dear was his life, but dearer still his fame!
When suppliant prayers no pardon could obtain,
And, wonderous strange 1 ev'n BEDFORD'S gold prov'd vain,
The informer's part her generous soul abhorr'd,
Though life preserv'd had been the sure reward;
Let impious ESCRICK act such treacherous scenes,
And shrink from death by such opprobrious means.

O! my lov'd RACHEL! all-accomplish'd fair!
Source of my joy, and soother of my care!
Whose heavenly virtues, and unfading charms,
Have bless'd through happy years my peaceful arms!
Parting with thee into my cup was thrown,
Its harshest dregs else had not forc'd a groan!—
But all is o'er—these eyes have gaz'd their last
And now the bitterness of death is past.

BURNET and TILLOTSON, with pious care,
My fleeting soul for heavenly bliss prepare,
Wide to my view the glorious realms display,
Pregnant with joy, and bright with endless day.
Charm'd, as of old when Israel's prophet sung,
Whose words distill'd like manna from his tongue,
While the great bard sublimest truths explor'd,
Each ravish'd hearer wonder'd and ador'd;
So rapt, so charm'd, my soul begins to rise,
Spurns the base earth, and seems to reach the skies.

But when descending from the sacred theme,
Of boundless power, and excellence supreme,
They would for man, and his precarious throne,
Exact obedience, due to Heaven alone,
Forbid resistance to his worst commands,
And place God's thunderbolts in mortal hands;
The vision sinks to life's contracted span,
And rising passion speaks me still a man.

What! shall a tyrant trample on the laws,
And stop the source whence all his power he draws?
His country's rights to foreign foes betray,

Lavish her wealth, yet stipulate for pay ?
To shameful falshoods venal slaves suborn,
And dare to laugh the virtuous man to scorn ?
Deride Religion, Justice, Honor, Fame,
And hardly know of Honesty the name ?
In Luxury's lap lie screen'd from cares and pains,
And only toil to forge his subjects chains ?
And shall he hope the public voice to drown,
The voice which gave, and can resume his crown !

When Conscience bares her horrors, and the dread
Of sudden vengeance, bursting o'er his head,
Wrings his black soul; when injured nations groan,
And cries of millions shake his tottering throne;
Shall flattering churchmen soothe his guilty ears,
With tortured texts, to calm his growing fears ;
Exalt his power above the aetherial climes,
And call down Heaven to sanctify his crimes !

O! impious doctrine!—Servile priests away !
Your Prince you poison, and your God betray.

Hapless the Monarch ! who, in evil hour,
Drinks from your cup the draught of lawless power !
The magic potion boils within his veins,
And locks each sense in adamantine chains;
Reason revolts, insatiate thirst ensues,
The wild delirium each fresh draught renews;
In vain his people urge him to refrain,
His faithful servants supplicate in vain;
He quaffs at length, impatient of control,
The bitter dregs that lurk within the bowl.

Ztal your pretence, but wealth and power you aims,
You ev'n could make a SOLOMON of JAMES.
Behold the pedant, thron'd in awkward state,
Absorb'd in pride, ridiculously great;
His courtiers seem to tremble at his nod,
His prelates call his voice the yoke of God;
Weakness and vanity with them combine,
And JAMES believes his majesty divine.
Presumptuous wretch I almighty power to scan,
While every action proves him less than man.

By your delusions to the scaffold led,
Martyr'd by you, a royal CHARLES has bled.
Teach then, ye sycophants! O! teach his son,
The gloomy paths of tyranny to shun ;
Teach him to prize Religion's sacred claim,
Teach him how Virtue leads to honest fame,
How Freedom's wreath a monarch's brows adorns,
Nor, basely fawning, plant his couch with thorns.
Point to his view his people's love alone,
The solid basis of his stedfast throne;
Chosen by them their dearest rights to guard,
The bad to punish, and the good reward,
Clement and just let him the sceptre sway,
And willing subjects shall with pride obey,
Shall vie to execute his high commands,
His throne their hearts, his sword and shield their hands.

Happy the Prince! thrice firmly fix'd his crown !
Who builds on public good his chaste renown;
Studious to bless, who knows no second aim,
His people's interest, and his own the same;
The ease of millions rests upon his cares,

And thus Heaven's high prerogative he shares.
Wide from the throne the blest contagion spreads,
O'er all the land its gladdening influence sheds,
Facction's discordant sounds are heard no more,
And foul Corruption flies the indignant shore.

His ministers with joy their courses run,
And borrow lustre from the royal sun.

But should some upstart, train'd in Slavery's school,
Learn'd in the maxims of despotic rule,
Full fraught with forms, and grave pedantic pride,
(Mysterious cloak! the mind's defects to hide!)
Sordid in small things, prodigal in great,
Saving for minions, squandering for the state
Should such a miscreant, born for England's bane,
Obscure the glories of a prosperous reign;
Gain, by the semblance of each praiseful art,
A pious prince's unsuspecting heart ;
Envious of worth, and talents not his own,
Chase all experienc'dmerit from the throne;
To guide the helm a motley crew compose,
Servile to him, the king's and country's foes;
Meanly descend each paltry place to fill,
With tools of power, and panders to his will;
 Brandishing high the scorpion scourge o'er all,
Except such slaves as bow the knee to Baal
Should Albion's fate decree the baneful hour—
Short be the date of his detested power!
Soon may his sovereign break his iron rods,
And hear his people; for their voice is God's!

Cease then your wiles, ye fawiling courtiers! cease,

Suffer your rulers to repose in peace;
By Reason led, give proper names to things,
God made them men, the people made them kings:
To all their acts but legal powers belong,
Thus England's Monarch never can do wrong;
Of right divine let foolish FILMER dream,
The public welfare is the law supreme.

Lives there a wretch, whose base, degenerate soul
Can crouch beneath a tyrant's stern control?
Cringe to his nod, ignobly kiss the hand
In galling chains that binds his native land?
Purchased by gold, or aw'd by slavish fear,
Abandon all his ancestors held dear?
Tamely behold that fruit of glorious toil,
England's Great Charter made a ruffian's spoil;
Hear, unconcern'd, his injured country groan,
Nor stretch an arm to hurl him from the throne?
Let such to freedom forfeit all their claims,
And CHARLES'S minions be the slaves of JAMES.

But soft awhile Now CAVENDISH, attend
The warm effusions of thy dying friend;
Fearless who dares his inmost thoughts reveal,
When thus to Heaven he makes his last appeal.
All-gracious Cod I whose goodness knows no bounds!
Whose power the ample universe surrounds!
In whose great balance, infinitely just.
Kings are but men, and men are only dust;
At thy tribunal low thy suppliant falls,
And here condemn'd, on thee for mercy calls!

Thou hear'st not, Lord! an hypocrite complain,

And sure with thee hypocrisy were vain;
To thy all-piercing eye the heart lies bare,
Thou know'st my sins, and, knowing, still canst spare)
Though partial power its ministers may awe,
And murder here by specious forms of law;
The axe, which executes the harsh decree,
But wounds the flesh, to set the spirit free!
Well may the man a tyrant's frown despise,
Who, spurning earth, to Heaven for refuge flies;
And on thy mercy, when his foes prevail,
Builds his firm trust; that rock can never fail!

Hear then, Jehovah! hear thy servant's prayer!
Be England's welfare thy peculiar care!
Defend her laws, her worship chaste, and pure,
And guard her rights while Heaven and Earth endure!
O let not ever fell Tyrannic Sway
His bloodstained standard on her shores display!
Nor fiery Zeal usurp thy holy name,
Blinded with blood, and wrapt in rolls of flame.
In vain let Slavery shake her threatening chain,
And Persecution wave her torch in vain!
Arise, O Lord! and hear thy people's call!
Nor for one man let three great kingdoms fall!

O! that my blood may glut the barbarous rage
Of freedom's foes, and England's ills assuage!
Grant but that prayer, I ask for no repeal,
A willing victim for my country's weal!
With rapturous joy the crimson stream shall flow,
And my heart leap to meet the friendly blow!

But should the fiend, tho' drench'd with human gore,

Dire Bigotry, insatiate, thirst for more,
And, arn'd from Rome, seek this devoted land,
Death in her eye, and bondage in her hand—
Blast her fell purpose! blast her foul desires!
Break .short her sward, and quench her horrid fires !

Raise up some champion, zealous to maintain
The sacred compat, by which monarchs reign !
Wise to foresee all danger from afar,
And brave to meet the thunders of the war!
Let pure religion, not to forms confin'd,
And love of freedom fill his generous mind !
Warm let his breast with sparks coelestial glow,
Benign' to man, the tyrant's deadly foe !
While sinking nations rest upon his arm,
Do thou the great Deliverer shield from harm !
Inspire his councils! aid his righteous sword!
Till Albion rings with Liberty restored!
Thence let her years in bright succession run!
And Freedom reign coeval with the sun.

'Tis done, my CA'NDISH, Heaven has heard my prayer;
So speaks my heart, for all is rapture there.

To Belgia's coast advert thy ravish'd eyes,
That happy coast, whence all our hopes arise!
Behold the Prince, perhaps thy future king !
From whose green years maturest blessings spring;
Whose youthful arm, when all-o'erwhelming
Power Ruthless march'd forth, his country to devour,
With finnbrac'dnerve repell'd the brutal force,
And stopp'd th' unwieldy giant in his course.

Great William hail 1 who sceptres could despise,
And spurn a crown with unretorted eyes!
O! when will princes learn to copy thee,
And leave mankind, as Heaven ordain'd them, free !

Haste, mighty Chief! our injur'd rights restore!
Quick spread thy sails for Albion's longing shore!
Haste, mighty Chief! ere millions groan enslav'd;
And add three realms to one already saved!
While Freedom lives, thy memory shall be dear,
And reap fresh honors each returning year;
Nations preserv'd shall yield immortal fame,
And endless ages bless thy glorious name !

Then shall my CA'NDISH, foremost in the field,
By justice arm'd, his sword conspicuous wield;
While willing legions crowd around his car,
And rush impetuous to the righteous war.
On that great day be every chance defied,
And think thy RUSSELL combats by thy side;
Nor, crown'd withvictory, cease thy generous toil,
Till firmest peace secure this happy isle.

Ne'er let thine honest, open heart believe
Professions specious, forg'd but to deceive;
Fear may extort them, when resources fail,
But O! reject the baseless, flattering tale.

Think not that promises, or oaths can bind,
With solemn ties, a Rome-devoted mind;
Which yields to all the holy juggler saith,
And deep imbibes the bloody, damning faith.
What though the Bigot raise to Heaven his eyes,

And call the Almighty witness from the skies!
Soon as the wish'd occasion he explores,
To plant the Roman cross on England's shores,
All, all will vanish, while his priests applaud,
And saint the perjurer for the pious fraud.

Far let him fly these freedom-breathing climes,
And seek proud Rome, the fosterer of his crimes;
There let him strive to mount the Papal chair,
And scatter empty thunders in the air,
Grimly preside in Superstition's school,
And curse those kingdoms he could never rule.

Here let me pause, and bid the world adieu.
While Heaven's bright mansions open to my view!—

Yet still one care, one tender care remains;
My bounteous friend, relieve a father's pains!
Watch o'er my Son, inform his waxen youth,
And mould his mind to virtue and to truth;
Soon let him learn fair liberty to prize,
And envy him, who for his country dies;
In one short sentence to comprize the whole,
Transfuse to his the virtues of thy soul.

Preserve thy life, my too, too generous friend,
Nor seek with mine thy happier fate to blend!
Live for thy country, live to guard her laws,
Proceed, and prosper in the glorious cause;
While I, though vanquish'd, scorn the field to fly,
But boldly face my foes, and bravely die.

Let princely MONMOUTH courtly wiles beware,

Nor trust too far to fond paternal care;
Too oft dark deeds deform the midnight cell,
Heaven only knows how noble ESSEX fell!
SIDNEY yet lives, whose comprehensive mind
Ranges at large through systems unconfined;
Wrapt in himself, he scorns the tyrant's power,
And hurls defiance even from the Tower;
With tranquil brow awaits the unjust decree,
And, arm'd with virtue, looks to follow me.

CA'NDISH, farewell! may Fame our names entwine!
Through life I lov'd thee, dying I am thine;
With pious rites let dust to dust be thrown,
And thus inscribe my monumental stone.

" Here RUSSEL lies, enfranchised by the grave,
Hepriz'd his birthright, nor would live a slave.
Few were his words, but honest and sincere,

Dear were his friends, his country still more dear;
In parents, children, wife, supremely bless'd,
But that one passion swallow'd all the rest;
To guard her freedom was his only pride,
Such was his love, and for that love he died."

Yet fear not Thou, when Liberty displays
Her glorious flag, to steer his course to praise;
For know, (whoe'er thou art that read'st his fate,
And think'st, perhaps, his sufferings were too great,)
Bless'd as he was, at her imperial call,
Wife, children, parents, he resign'd them all;
Each, fond affection then forsook his soul,
And AMOR PATRIAE occupied the whole;

In that great cause he joy'd to meet his doom,
Bless'd the keen axe, and triumph'd o'er the tomb.

The hour draws near—But what are hours to me?
Hours, days, and years hence undistinguished flee!
Time, and his glass unheeded pass away,
Absorb'd, and lost in one vast flood of day!
On Freedom's wings my soul is borne on high,
And soars exulting to its native sky!

EPISTLE VII.

ARISBE
TO THE YOUNGER
MARIUS.

LORDHERVEY.

OF all I valued, all I lov'd, bereft,
Say, has my heart this little comfort left?
That you the mem'ry of its truth retain,
And think with grateful pity on my pain?
Though but with life my sorrows can have end,
(For death alone can join me to my Friend)
Yet think not I repent I set you free,
I mourn your absence, not your liberty.

Before my Marius left Numidia's coast,
Each day I saw him; scarce an hour was lost:
Now months and years must pass, nay life shall prove
But one long absence from the man I love.
Yourself I lost: oh! grateful, then confess,
My trial greater, though my glory less.

Yes, partial gods! inflicters of my care!
Be witness what I felt, what grief, what fear!
When full of stifled woes the night he fled,
' No sigh I dar'd o'breathe, no tear to shed.
Whilst men of faith approv'd, a chosen crew,
Firm to their trust, and to their mistress true,
With care too punctual my commands obey,
And in one freight my life and thee convey.
The harder task was mine; condemn'd to bear,
With brow serene, my agonizing care;
To mix an idle talk, to force a smile,
A king and jealous lover to beguile.
Think in that dreadful interval of fate,
All I held dear, thy safety in debate,
Think what I suffer'd, whilst my heart afraid
Suggests a thousand times, that all's betray'd.
A thousand times revolving in 'my mind
The doubtful chance; oh! Love ! said I, be kind:
Propitious to my scheme, thy vot'ry aid,
And be my fondness by success repaid.
Now bolder grown, with sanguine hopes elate,
My fancy represents thy smiling fate;
The guards deceived, and every danger o'er,
The winds already waft him from the shore.
These pleasing images anew impart
Life to,my eyes, and gladness to my heart;
Dispel the gloomy fears that cloud my face,
And charm the little flutterer to peace.
But now the king, or tasteless to my charms,
Or weary of an absent mistress' arms,
His own apartment seeks, and grateful rest;
Thar courted stranger to the careful breast.
Whilst I, by hopes and fears alternate sway'd,

Impatient ask the slaves if I'm obey'd.
'Tis done, they cry'd, and struck me with despair;
For what I long'd to know, I dy'd to hear.
Fantastic turn of a distracted mind;
I blam'd the gods for having been too kind;
Curs'd the success they granted to my vows,
And this assistant hand that fill'd my woes.
Such was my frenzy in that hour of care,
And such'th' injustice of my bold despair;
That even those, ungrateful, I upbraid,
Whose fatal diligence my will obey'd.
Scarce, Marius, did thyself escape my rage;
(Most lov'd of men!) when fears of black presage
Describe thy hand so fond of liberty,
It never gave one parting throb for me.
At every step you should have turn'd your eye,
"Dropt a regretful tear, and heav'd a sigh;
The nature of the grace I shew'd was such,
You not deserv'd it, if it pleas'd too much.
A lover would have linger'd as he fled,
And oft in anguish to himself have said,
Farewell forever! Ah! yet more had done,
A lover never would have fled alone.
To force me from a hated rival's bed, ...
Why comes not Marius at an army's head?
Oh! did thy heart but wish to see that day,
'Twould all my past, and future woes o'erpay.

But vain are all these hopes: preserve thy breast
From falsehood only, I forgive the rest
Too happy, if no envy'd rival boast
Those joys Arisbe to her Marius lost.

EPISTLE VIII.

FLORA TO POM PET.

By the Same.

ERE death these closing eyes for ever shade
(That death thy cruelties have welcome made),
Receive, thou yet lov'd Man! this one adieu,
This last farewell to happiness and you.
My eyes o'erflow with tears, my trembling hand
Can scarce the letters form, or pen command;
The dancing paper swims before my sight,
And scarce myself can read the words I write.

Think you behold me in this lost estate,
And think yourself the author of my fate :
How vast the change! your Flora's now become
The general pity, not the boast of Rome.
This form, a pattern to the sculptor's art,
This face, the idol once of Pompey's heart,
(Whose picctur'd beauties Rome thought fit to place
The sacred temples of her gods to grace)
Are charming now no more; the bloom is fled,
The lilies languid, and the roses dead.
Soon shall some hand the glorious work deface,
Where Grecian pencils tell what Flora was:
No longer my resemblance they impart,
They lost their likeness, when I lost thy heart.

O! that those hours could take their turn again

When Pompey, lab'ring with a jeaLouspain,
His Flora thus bespoke: " Say, my dear love!.
Shall all these rivals unsuccessful prove ?
In vain, for ever, shall the Roman youth
Envy my happiness, and tempt thy truth ?
Shall neither tears nor prayers thy pity move ?
Ah! give not pity, 'tis a-kin to love.
Would Flora were not fair in such excess,
That I might fear, though not adore her less."

Fool that I was, I sought to ease that grief,
Nor knew indifference follow'd the relief:
Experience taught the cruel truth too late,
I never dreaded, 'till I found my fate.
'Twas mine to ask if Pompey's self could hear,
Unmov'd, his rival's unsuccessful pray'r;
To make thee swear he'd not thy pity move :
Alas! such pity is no kin to love.
You chid my faith, reproach'd my being true,
(Unnat'ral thought !) and labor'd to subdue
The constancy my soul maintained for you;
To other arms your mistress you condemn'd,
Too cool a lover, and too warm a friend.

How could'st thou thus my lavish heart abuse,
To ask the only thing it could refuse ?
Nor yet upbraid me, Pompey, what I say,
For 'tis my merit that I can't obey;
Yet this alleg'd against me as a fault,
Thy rage fomented, and my ruin wrought.
Just Gods 1 what tie, what conduct can prevail
O'er fickle man, when truth like mine can fail ?

Urge not, to gloss thy crime, the name of friend,
We know how far those sacred laws extend;
Since other heroes have not blush'd to prove
How weak all passions when oppos'd to love:
Nor boast the virtuous conflict of thy heart,
When gen'rous pity took Geminius' part;
Tis all heroic fraud, and Roman art.
Such flights of honor might amuse the crowd,
But by a mistress ne'er can be allow'd;
Keep for the senate, and the grave debate,
That infamous hypocrisy of state,
There wosds are virtue, and your trade deceit.

No riddle is thy change, nor hard t' explain,
Flora was fond, and Pompey was a man;
No longer then a specious tale pretend,
Nor plead fictitious merit to your friend .
By nature false, you follow'd her decree,
Nor gen'rous are to him, but false to me.

You say you melted at Geminius' tears,
You say you felt his agonizing cares:
Gross artifice! that this from him could move,
And not from Flora, whom you say you love;
You could not bear to hear your rival sigh,
Yet bear unmov'd to see your mistress die.
Inhuman hypocrite' not thus can he
My wrongs, and my distress, obdurate, see.

He, who receiv'd, condemns the gift you made,
And joins with me the giver to upbraid,
Forgetting he's oblig'd, and mourning I'm betray'd
He loves too well that cruel gift to use,

Which Pompey lov'd too little to refuse :
Fain would he call my vagrant lord again,
But I. the kind ambassador "restrain ;
I scorn to let another take my part,
And to myself will owe or lose thy heart.

Can nothing e'er rekindle love in thee ?
Can nothing e'er extinguish it in me ?
That I could tear thee from this injur'd breast ?
And where you gave my person, give the rest,
At once to grant and punish thy request.
That I could place thy worthy rival there !
No second insult need my fondness fear:
He views not Flora with her Pompey's eyes,
He loves like me, he doats, despairs, and dies.

Come to my arms, thou dear deserving youth!,
Thou prodigy of man 1 thou man with truth!
For him, I will redouble every care,
To please, for him, these faded charms repair;
To crown his vows, and sharpen thy despair.

Oh ! 'tis illusion all ! and idle rage !
No second passion can this heart engage;
And shortly, Pompey, shall thy Flora prove,
Death may dissolve, but nothing change her love.

EPISTLE IX.

ROXANA TO USBECK.

By the Same.

THINK not I write my innocence to prove,
To sue for pity, or awake thy love;
No mean defence expect, or abject prayers;
Thou know'st no mercy, and I know no tears:
I laugh at all thy vengeance has decreed,
Avow the fact, and glory in the deed.

Yes, Tyrant 1 I deceiv'd thy spies and thee:
Pleas'd in oppression, and in bondage free:
The rigid agents of thy cruel laws
By gold I won to aid my juster cause:
With extrous skill eluded all thy care,
And acted more than jealousy could fear;
To wanton bow'rs this prison-house I turn'd,
And bless'd that absence which you thought mourn'd.
But short those joys allow'd by niggard Fate,
Yet so refin'd, so exquisitely great,
That their excess compensated their date.
I die: already in each burning vein
I feel the pois'nous draught and bless the pain:
For what is life unless its joys we prove?
And where is joy, depriv'd of what we love.

Yet, ere I die) this justice I have paid
To my dear murder'd lover's injur'd shade:

Those sacrilegious instruments of power,
Who wrought that ruin these sad eyes deplore,
Already with their blood their crimes atone,
And for his life have sacrific'd their own.

Thee, though restraint and absence may defend
From my revenge, my curses still attend:
Despair like mine, Barbarian! be thy part,
Remorse afflict, and sorrow sting thy heart.

Nor think this hate commencing in my breast,
Though prudence long its latent force suppressed;
I knew those wrongs that I was forc'd to bear,
And curs'd those chains injustice made me wear.

For could'st thou hope Roxana to deceive
With idle tales, which only fools believe?
Poor abject souls in superstition bred,
In ign'rance train'd, by prejudice misled;
Whom hireling dervises by proxy teach
From those whose false prerogative they preach.
Didst thou imagine me so weak of mind,
Because I murmur'd not, I ne'er repin'd,
But hugg'd my chain, and thought my jailor kind
That willingly those laws I,e'er obey'd,
Which Pride invented, and Oppression made?
And whilst self-licens'd through the world you
To quicken appetite by change in love;
Each passion sated, and each wish possess'd
Which Lust can urge, or Fancy can suggest:
That I should mourn thy loss with fond regret,
Weap the misfortune, and the wrong forget?

Could I believe that Heav'n this beauty gave,
(Thy transient pleasure, and thy lasting slave;)
Indu'd with reason, only to fulfil
The harsh commands of thy capricious will?
No, Usbeck, no, my soul disdain'd those laws;
And, though I wanted pow'r t'assert my cause,
My right I knew; and still those pleasures sought
Which Justice warranted, and Nature taught :
On Custom's senseless precepts I refin'd,
I weigh'd what Heav'n, I knew what man design'd
And form'd by her own rules my free-born mind.

Thus whilst this wretched body own'd thy pow'
Doom'd, unredress'd, its hardships to deplore;
My soul subservient to herself alone,
And Reason independent on her throne,
Contemn'd thy dictates, and obey'd their own.
Yet thus far to my conduct thanks are due,
At least I condescended to seem true;
Endeavored still my sentiments to hide,
Indulg'd thy vanity, and sooth'd thy pride.
Though this submission to a tyrant paid,
Whom not my duty, but my fears obey'd,
If rightly weigh'd, would more deserve the blame,
Who call it Virtue, but prophane her name;
For to the world, I should have own'd that love,
Which all impartial judges must approve:
You urg'd a right to tyrannize my heart,
Which he, soliciting, assail'd by art,
Whilst I, impatient of the name of slave,
To force refus'd, what I to merit gave.

Oft, as thy slaves this wrethed body led

To the detested pleasures of thy bed;
In those soft moments, consecrate to joy, —
Which ecstasy and transport should employ;
Clasp'd in your arms, you wonder'd still to find
So col'd. my kisses, so compos'd my mind:
But had thy cheated eyes discern'd aright,
You'd found aversion, where you sought delight.

Not that my soul, incapable of love,
No charms could warm, no tenderness could move;
For him, whose love my every thought possess'd,
A fiercer passion fill'd this constant breast,
Than truth e'er felt, or falshood e'er possess'd.

This style unusual to thy pride appears,
For truths a stranger to the tyrant's ears.
But what have I to manage, or to dread?
Nor threats alarm, nor insults hurt the dead:
No wrongs they feel, no miseries they find;
Cares are the legacies we leave behind:
In the calm grave no Usbecks we deplore,
No tyrant husband, no oppressive pow'r.
Alas! I faint—Death intercepts the rest:
The venom'd drug is busy in my breast:
Each nerve's unstrung: a mist obscures the day:
My senses, strength, and ev'n my hate decay;
Though rage awhile the ebbing spirits stay'd,
Tis past—they sink beneath the transient aid.
Take then, inhuman Wretch! my last farewell;
Pain be thy portion here! hereafter, hell!
And when our Prophet shall my fate decree,
Be any curse my punishment, but Thee!

EPISTLE X.

MONIMIJ TO PHILOCLES.

By the Same.

SINCE language never can describe my pain,
How can I hope to move when I complain?
But such is woman's frenzy in distress,
We love to plead, though hopeless of redress.

Perhaps, affecting ignorance, thou'lt say,
From whence these lines? whose message to convey
Mock not my grief with that feign'd cold demand,
Too well you know the hapless writer's hand:
But if you force me to avow my shame,
Behold it prefac'd with Moninu's name.

Lost to the world, abandon'd and forlorn,
Expos'd to infamy, reproach and scorn,
To mirth and comfort lost, and all for you,
Yet lost, perhaps, to your remembrance too;
How hard my lot! what refuge can I try,
Weary of life, and yet afraid to die!
Of hope, the wretch's last resort, bereft,
By Friends, by Kindred, by my Lover, left!
Oh! frail dependence of confiding fools 1
On lovers' oaths, or friendship's sacred rules,
How weak in modern hearts, too late I find,
Monimia's fall'n, and Philocles unkind!
To these reflections, each slow wearing day,

And each revolving night a constant prey,
Think what I suffer, nor ungentle hear
What madness dictates in my fond despair;
Grudge not this short relief, (too fast it flies)
Nor chide that weakness I myself despise.
One moment sure may be at least her due,
Who sacrific'd her all of life for you.
Without a frown this farewell then receive,
For tis the last my hapless love shall give;
Northis I would, if reason could command :
But what restriction reins a lover's hand ?
Nor prudence, shame, nor pride, nor int'res sways,
The hand implicitly the heart obeys:
Too well this maxim has my conduct shewn,
Too well that conduct to the world is known.

Oft have I writ, and often to the flame
Condemn'dthis after-witness of my shame;

Oft in my cooler recollected thought,
Thy beauties, and my fondness half forgot.
(How short those intervals for reason's aid!)
Thus to myself in anguish have I said.

Thy vain remonstrance, foolish maid, give o'er,
Who act the wrong, can ne'er that wrong deplore.
Then sanguine hopes again delusive reign,
I form'd thee melting, as I tell my pain.
If not of rock thy flinty heart is made,
Nor tigers nurs'd thee in the desart shade,
Let me at least thy cold compassion prove,
That slender sustenance of greedy loys;
Though no return my warmer wishes find,

Be to the wretch, though not the mistress, kind;
Nor whilst I court my melancholy state,
Forget 'twas love, and thee, that wrought my fate.
Without, restraint habituate to range
The paths of pleasure, can I bear this change
Doom'd from the world unwilling to retire,
In bloom of life, and warm with young desire,
In lieu of roofs with regal splendor gay,
Condemn'd in distant wilds to drag the day;
Where beasts of prey maintain their savage court,
Or human brutes (the worst of brutes) resort.
Yes, yes, the change I could unsighing see,
For none I mourn, but what I find in thee,
There centre all my woes, thy heart estrang'd,
I weep my lover, not my fortune, chang'd;
Bless'd with thy presence, I could all forget,
Nor gilded palaces in huts regret,
But exil'd thence, superfluous is the rest,
Each place the same, my hell is in my breast;
To pleasure dead, and living but to pain,
My only sense to suffer, and complain.

As all my wrongs distressful I repeat,
Say, can thy pulse with equal cadence beat?
Canst thou know peace? is conscience mute within?
That upright delegate for secret sin:
Is nature so extinguish'd in thy heart,
That not one spark remains to take my part?
Not one repentant throb, one grateful sigh?
Thy breast unruffled, and un wet thy eye?
Thou cool betrayer, temperate in ill!
Thou nor remorse, nor thought humane canst feel:
Nature has form'd thee of the rougher kind,

And education more debas'd thy mind,
Born in an age when guilt and fraud prevail,
When Justice sleeps, and Int'rest holds"the scale;
Thy loose companions, a licentious crew,
Most to each other, all to us untrue,
Whomchance, or habit mix, but rarely choice,
Nor leagu'din friendship, but in social vice,
Who indigent of honor, or of shame,
Glory in crimes which others blush to name;
By right or wrong disdaining to be mov'd,
Unprincipled, unloving, and unlov'd.
The fair who trusts their prostituted vows,
If not their falshood, still their boasts expose;
Nor knows the wisest to elude the harm,
Ev'n she whose prudence shuns the tinsel charn,
They know to slander, though they fail to warm:
They make her languish in fictitious flame,
Affix some specious slander on her name,
And, baffled by her virtue, triumph o'er her fame.
These are the leaders of thy blinded youth,
These vile seducers laugh'd thee out of truth;
Whose scurril jests all solemn ties profane,
Or Friendship's band, or Hymen's sacred chain;
Morality as weakness they upbraid, ,
Norev'n revere Religion's hallow'd head ;
"Alike they spurn divine and human laws,
And treat the honest like the christian cause.
Curse on that tongue whose vile pernicious art
Delights the ear but to corrupt the heart,
That takes advantage of the chearful hour, —
When weaken'd Virtue bends to Nature's'power,
And would the goodness of the soul efface,
To substitute dishonor in her place.

With such you lose the day in false delights,
In lewd debauch you revel out the nights,
(O fatal commerce to Monimia's peace !)
Their arguments convince because they please;
While sophistry for reason they admit,
And wander dazzled by the glare of wit,
Wit that on ill a specious lustre throws, .
And in false colors every object shows,
That gilds the wrong, depreciating the right,
And hurts the judgment, while it feasts the sight;
So in a prism to the deluded eye
Each picur'd trifle takes a rainbow dye,
With borrow'd charms the shining prospect glows,
And truth reversed the faithless mirror shows,
Inverted scenes in bright confusion lie,
The Jawns impending o'er the nether sky;
No just, no real images we meet,
But all the gaudy vision is deceit.

Oft I revolve in this distracted mind
Each word, each look, that spoke my charmer kine
But oh ! how dear their memory I pay!
What pleasures past can present cares allay?
Of all I love for ever dispossess'd:
Ah! what avails to think I once was bless'd ?
Hard disposition of unequal fate !
Mix'd arc our joys, and transient are their date;
Nor can reflection bring them back again,
Yet brings an after-sting to every pain.

Thy fatal, letters, oh immoral Youth,
Those perjur'd pledges of fictitious truth,

Dear as they were no second joy afford,
My credulous heart once leap'd at every word,
My glowing bosom throbb'd with thick-heav'd sigh
And-floods of rapture gush'd into my eyes:
When now repeated (for thy theft was vain,
Each treasur'd syllable my thoughts retain)
Far other passions rule, and diff'rent care,
My joys and grief, my transport and despair.

Why dost thou mock the ties of constant love !
But half its joys the faithless ever prove,
They only taste the pleasures they receive,
When sure the noblest is in those we give.
Acceptance is the heav'n which mortals know;
But 'tis the bliss of Angels to bestow.
Oh! emulate, my Love, that task divine,
Be thou that Angel, and that heav'n be mine.
Yet, yet relent, yet intercept my fate;
Alas! I rave, and sue for new deceit.
As soom the dead shall from the grave return,
As love extinguish'd with new ardor burn.
Oh! that I dar'd to act a Roman part,
And stab thy image in this faithful heart,
Where riveted for life secure you reign,
A cruel inmate, author of my pain :
But coward-like irresolute I wait
Time's tardy aid, nor dare to rush on fate;
Perhaps may linger out life's latest stage,
Survive thy cruelties, and fall by age:
No—grief shall swell my sails, and speed me o'er
(Despair my pilot) to that quiet shore
Where I can trust, and thou betray no more.
Might I but once again behold thy charms,

Might I but breathe my last in those dear arms,
On that lov'd face but fix my closing eye,
Permitted, where I might not live, to die;
My soften'd fate I would accuse no more:
But fate has no such happiness in store!
'Tis past, 'tis done—what gleam of hope behind,
When I can ne'er be false, nor thou be kind?
Why then this care?—-'tis weak—'tis vain—farewell—
At that last word what agonies I feel!
I faint-r-I die—remember I was true
'Tis all I ask—eternally—adieu!—

EPISTLE XL

FROM
MISS—

TO THE
EARL OF —

AND dar'st thou then, insulting Lord! demand
A friendly answer from this trembling hand?—
No more thy tears my tender page shall stain,
Ambiguous tears, dissembling joy or pain;
No more thine eyes with sweet surprize pursue
Love's sacred mysteries, there unveil'd to you.
Demand'st thou still an answer? let it be
An answer worthy vengeance, worthy me!
Hear it, in public characters, relate
An ill- starr'd passion, and capricious fate:
Yes, public let it stand! to warn the maid
From one who fell less vanquished than betray'd;
Guiltless, yet doom'd with guilty pangs to groan,

And expiate others' treasons, not her own;
Destin'd with shame in Honor's paths to run;
Still Virtue's follower, yet by Vice undone.
Such free complaint to injur'd Love belongs :—
Yes, tyrant, read, and know me by my wrongs !
Yes, traitor, read, and reading tremble too!
I come to blaze thee to a nation's view ;
I come—ah, wretch, thy swelling rage control!
Was he not once the idol of thy soul ?
True, by his guilt thy tortur'd bosom bleeds,
Yet spare the guilty—for 'tis Love that pleads:
Respecting him, respecl thy infant flame;
Proclaim the treason, hide the traitor's name !
Enough to Honor and Revenge is given,
This truth reserve for Conscience, and for Heaven !

Talk'st thou, ingrate! of Friendship's holy powers ?
The tiger's union with the lamb be ours!
This cold, this frozen bosom, didst thou dream,
Senseless to love, shall soften to esteem ?
What means thy friendship shall I bless my fate,
Losing thy love, to just escape thy hate
Remember thee !repeat that sound again:
My heart applauding echoes to the strain.
Yes, till this heart forgets to beat and grieve,
Live there thy image—but detested live !
My hate pursue thee, wmmpar'd by age,
Nor memory waken, but to kindle rage.
Enter thy treacherous boson,enter deep;
Hear Conscience call, white flattering passions sleep!
Where harbour Honor, Conscience, Faith and Truth;
Where the bright forms whose semblance caught my youth ?
How could I doubt thy noble breast their shrine,

That felt them glowing, tender maid! in mine.
Boast not of trophies from my fall achiev'd !
Boast not, deceiver, of this soul deceiv'd !
Easy the traitor wins an open heart,
Artless itself, and unsuspecting art;
Not by superior wiles successful proves,
But fond credulity in her who loves.

Blush, shameless grandeur, blush I shall BRITAIN'S PEER,
Daring all crimes, not dare to be sincere ?
What charms were mine, to tempt thy guilty fires ?
What wealth, what honors from illustrious sires ?
Can virtue's simple spoils adorn thy race ?
Shall annals mark a village maid's disgrace ?
When bursting tears my inward anguish speak,
When paleness spreads my sometimes flushing cheek
When my frame trembles with convulsive strife,
My spirits flutter on the verge of life;
When to my heart my ebbing pulse is driven,
My eyes throw .faint accusing beams to heaven;
Yet griefs that freeze my accents, save my fame :—
Come, blast it, traitor !—no; the tale of shame,
The guilty tale, unwilling lips confine—
My portion, misery; but no triumph thine !

Would thou hadst left me where I met thine eye,
A simple flower, to bloom in shades and die!
On downy wings where rose the sprightly morn,
Where evening found not in my breast a thorn;
Pure joys were mine; Content at least, that flows
With temperate current through this vale of woes,
Cruel, to poison moments sweet as these !
On me to practise fatal arts to please!

Destin'd, if prosperous, for sublimer charms,
To court proud Wealth and Greatness to thy arms.
How many a lighter, many a fairer dame,
Fond of her prize, had fann'd thy fickle flame;
With livelier moments sooth'd thy vacant mind,
Easy possessed thee, easy too resign'd;
Chang'd but her object, Passion's willing slave,
Nor felt the wound that festers to the grave!
Ah! had I, conscious of thy fierce desires,
But half consenting shar'd contagious fires,
Half yielding heard thine impious suit maintained,
This trembling heart had suffer'd, not complain'd!
But ah! with tears and crowded sighs to sue,
To dress dissembled passions like the true;
To borrow still Confusion's sweet disguise,
Meet my coy virtues with dejected eyes;
To steal their language which no words impart,
And give me back the image of my heart;
This, this was treachery:—by such arts assail'd,
I fell—Great God! what virtue had not fail'd!

Yet unrelenting still the tyrant cries,
Heedless of Pity's voice, and Beauty's sighs,
That pious frauds, the wisest, best, approve,
And Heaven but smiles at perjuries in love.
No; Heaven and Virtue scorn the mean pretence!
No;'tis the villain's, 'tis the slave's defence!
No; 'tis the base sensation cowards feel 1
The wretch who trembles at the brave man's steel
In woman's rage no daring mischief fears,
And mocks the feeble arms of sighs and tears.
In vain a sex, by nature taught to rest
Its trembling weakness on your firmer breast,

Pleads pity:—coward man, to woman brave,
Insults the virtue he was born to save.

What! shall the lightest promise lips can feign,
Bind man to man in Honor's sacred chain \
And oaths to us not sanctify th' accord,
Not heaven attested, nor heaven's awful Lord ?—
Why various laws for beings form'd the same ?
Equal from one indulgent power we came,
Who, blessing to be blest, design'd his race
With manly vigor tempering female grace.
Sequester'd from our sex, vain man, relate
Your solitary pleasure's sullen state!
What tender joys sit brooding o'er your store ?
What slumbers sooth Ambition bath'd in gore ?
'Tis ours, th' unsocial passions to control,
To pour the balm that heals the wounded soul;
To lure your fancy with diviner themes
Than Wealth, than Power's delusive restless dreams.
Yet frantic man, dissolving bonds so dear,
Secure from Love, his empire founds on Fear:
Nor dream'st thou, traitor, what confirms thy laws,
Not manly triumph—Blush to hear the cause!
'Tis female softness—Tyrants else might feel
The' desperate vengeance of a woman's steel.

Still if you glory in the lion's force,
Come, nobly emulate that lion's course !
From guarded herds he vindicates his prey,
Not lurks in thickets from the blaze of day;
While man, not confident in manly arms,
Now offering truce, now sounding false alarms,
With customs, laws, with' terror, fraud, combin'd,

Relaxes all the nerves that brace the mind,
Then lordly, savage, rends the trembling heart,
First gain'd by treachery, and then tam'd by art.

Are these reflections then that Love inspires?
Is bitter grief the fruit of fair desires?
From whose example could I dream to find
The mournful privilege to curse mankind?
Ah, long I strove to burst th' enchanting tye,
And form'd resolves that ev'n in forming die:
Too long! linger'd on the fatal coast,
And ey'd the ocean where my wealth was lost:
In silence wept, scarce venturing to complain;
Still to my heart dissembled half my pain:
Ascrib'd my sufferings to its fears, not you;
Beheld yon treacherous, and then wish'd you true.
Sooth'd by those wishes, by myself deceiv'd,
I fondly hop'd, and, hoping, I believ'd.—
Cruel! to whom, ah whither can 1 flee,
Friends, Fortune, Fame, deserted all for thee?
On whom but Thee this aching frame repose?
With whom but Thee deposit all its woes?
To whom, but Thee, explain its stifled groan,
And live for whom but Thee and Love alone?
What hand to probe my bleeding heart be found?
What hand to heal, but his that gave the wound?

O dreadful chaos! when the ruin'd mind, .
Lost to itself, to virtue, human-kind,
Prom earth to heaven, a meteor flaming wide,
Link'd to no system, to no world allied,
Feels all a blank within:—each pregnant thought
That Nature, Reason, that Experience taught,

Past, present, future, feels alike destroy'd,
While love alone usurps the mighty void !
A void how gloomy, when that Love is flown !
What shades we grasp, the noble substance gone!
From one ador'd, adoring once, we dream
Of Friendship's tenderness—ev'n cold Esteem.
Rejected, still the suppliant suit advance—
Plead for a last farewell—a moment's glance—
A letter—token—wreck'd in search of shore,
We catch the plank of Hope, and rise no more.
Pursued again a too successful theme,
And dry'd my eyes, with youre again to stream:
When praclis'd tears your venial fault confcst,
And half dissembled, half excus'd the rest,
To kindred griefs taught pity by my own,
Sighs I rerurn'd, and answer'd groan for groan;
Your self-reproaches, stifling mine, approv'd,
And much I credited, for much I lov'd.
Not long the soul this doubtful dream prolongs;
Pardoning indeed, but not forgetting wrongs,
It scorns the traitor, and with conscious pride
Scorns a base self-deserting to his side :
Great by misfortune, greater by despair,
Its heaven once lost, disdains an humbler care:
Perhaps too tender, or too fierce, my soul
Disclaiming half the heart, demands the whole.

I blame thee not, that, fickle as thy race,
New loves invite thee, and the old efface ;
That cold, insensible thy soul appears
To Virtue's smiles, to Virtue's very tears:—
But oh, a hearfrwhose tenderness you knew,
That held, frail tenure I life itself from you ;

In fond presumption that securely play'd,
Securely slumber'd in your friendly shade,
Whose every weakness, every sigh to share,
The powers that haunt the perjur'd, heard you swear,
Was this a heart you wantonly resign'd
Victim to scorn, to ruin, and mankind?
Was this—O traitor, that betray'st no more,
What means thy pity? what can vows restore?
Can vows recall th' autumnal year to bloom?
Or quicken ashes slumbering in the tomb?
Can vows to smiles relax the brow of Care,
Or heal thy scars of anguish, fierce Despair?
Bid Virtue's sullied flames again refine?
Or Honor visit a deserted shrine?
Ah no nor prayers, nor all th' immortal powers,
Back to their once-trod circles win the hours!
Cruel! no more thy flattering form betrays,
The feeble visjpn melts in Reason's rays.
Yet take my pardon in my last farewell—
Daggers, like those you planted, never fee!
Fated, like me, to curse, yet court your fate;
To blend, in dreadful union, Love and Hate;
Chiding the present moment's lingering haste,
To dread the future, and deplore the past;
Like me condemn th' effect, the cause approve,
Renounce the lover, yet retain the love!

Yes, Love! ev'n now, in this ill-fated hour,
An exile from thy joys, I feel thy power.
Yon orient sun, once lovely to my sight,
Bathing in vernal dews his youthful light,
Congenial to my griefs, now sullen glows:
The streams that murmur, yet not court repose;

The breezes sickening with my mind's disease,
And valleys laughing to all eyes but these,
Proclaim thy absence, Love! whose beam alone
Lighted my morn with glories not its own!
Ah, noblest passion life and youth impart,
Soon as thy flame shot rapture to my heart,
A new creation brighten'd on my view;
Nurs'd in thy smiles the social passions grew:
New strung, th' harmonious nerves, the thrilling veins,
Beat, in sweet unison, to others pains.
The blood, to partial currents once confin'd,
Now swell'd an ocean, and embrac'd mankind.
The soul, once centering in itself the blaze,
Now wide diffus'd Benevolence's rays;
Kindling on earth, pursu'd th' aethrial road,
In hallow'd flames ascending to its God.

Ah, Love!—in vain a blasting hand destroys
Thy swelling blossoms of expected joys;
Converts to poison what for food was given,
Thy manna dropping from its native heaven;
Victorious still thou triumph'st! still confest
The purest transport that can warm the breast—
Yes, traitor, yes:—my heart, to Nature true,
Adores the passion, and detests but you.

EPISTLE XII.
ABELARD TO ELOISA.

BY
W. PATTISON.

IN my dark cell, low prostrate on the ground,

Mourning my crimes, thy letter entrance found;
Too soon my soul the well-known name confest;
My beating heart sprung fiercely in my breast:
Thro' my whole frame a guilty transport glow'd,
And streaming torrents from my eyes fast flow'd.
O Eloisa! art thou still the same?
Dost thou still nourish this destructive flame?
Have not the gentle rules of peace and heaven
From thy soft soul this fatal passion driven?
Alas! I thought thee disengaged and free;
And can'st thou still, still sigh and weep for me i
What powerful deity, what hallow'd shrine,
Can save me from a love and faith like thine?
Where shall I fly, when not this awful cave,
Whose rugged feet the surging billows lave;
When not these gloomy cloister's solemn walls,
O'er whose rough sides the languid ivy crawls \
When my dread vows in vain their force oppose,
Opposed to love—alas! how vain are vows!
in fruitless penitence I wear away
Each tedious night; each sad revolving day
I fast, I pray; and, with deceitful art,
Veil thy dear image from my tortur'd heart:
My tortur'd heart conflicting passions move.
I hope, despair, repent—yet still I love.
A thousand jarring thoughts my bosom tear,
For thou, not God, O Eloise art there.
To the false world's deluding pleasures dead,
,Nor longer by its wandering fires misled,
In learn'd disputes harsh precepts I infuse,
And give that counsel I want power to use.
The rigid maxims of the grave and wise
Have quench'd each milder sparkle of my eyes;

Each lovely feature of this well-known face,
By grief revers'd, assumes a sterner grace.
O Eloisa! should the fetes once more,
Indulgent to my view, thy charms restore!
How wouldst thou from my arms with horror start,
To miss the form familiar to thy heart!
Nought could thy quick, thy piercing judgment see,
To speak thy Abelard—but love of thee.
Lean abstinence, pale grief, and haggard care,
The dire attendants of forlorn despair,
Have Abelard the young, the gay, rcmov'd,
And in the hermit sunk the man you lov'd.
Wrapt in the gloom these holy mansions shed,
The thorny paths of penitence I tread;
Lost to the world, from all its interests free,
And torn from all my soul held dear in thee.
Ambition, with its train of frailties gone,
All love, all forms forgot, but thirie alone.
Amid the blaze of day, the dusk of night,
My Eioisa rises to my sight:
Veil'd, as in Paraclete's secluded towers,
The wretched mourner counts the lagging hours;
I hear her sighs, see the swift-falling tears,
Weep all her griefs, and pine with all her cares.
O vOWS ! O convents! your stern force impart,
And town the melting phantom from my heart
Let other sighs a worthier sorrow show;
Let other tears, for sin, repentant flow :
Low to the earth my guilty eyes 1 roll,
And humble to the dust my contrite soul.
Forgiving Power! thy gracious call I meet,
Who first impower'd this rebel heart to beat;
Who thro' this trembling, this offending frame,

For nobler ends diffus'd life's active flame :
O change the temper of this laboring breast,
And form anew each beating pulse to rest!
Let springing grace, fair faith, and hope remove
@@@ fatal traces of destructive love;
Destructive love from its warm mansion tear,
And leave no tracks of Eioisa there.
Are these the wishes of my inmost soul ?
Would I its softest, tenderest sense control ?
Would I this touch'd, this glowing heart refine
To the cold substance of that marble shrine ?
Transform'd like these pale swarms that round me move
Of blest insensibles—who know not love ?
Ah! rather let me keep this hapless flame;
Adieu, false honor! unavailing fame!
Not your harsh rules, but tender love supplies
The streams that gush from my despairing eyes:
I feel the traitor melt around my heart,
And thro' my veins with treacherous influence dart.
Inspire me, Heaven ! assist me Grace divine!
Aid me, ye Saints! unknown to crimes like mine :
You who on earth serene all griefs could prove,
All but the torturing pangs of hopeless love :
A holier rage in your pure bosoms dwelt,
Nor can you pity what you never felt.
A sympathizing grief alone can cure;
The hand that heals must feel what I endure :
Thou Eloise alone canst give me ease, .
And bid my struggling soul subside to peace;
Restore me to my long-lost heaven of rest,
And take thyself from my reluctant breast.
If crimes like mine could an allay receive,
That blest allay thy wonderous charms must give t

Thy form, that first to love my heart inclined,
Still wanders in my lost, my guilty mind :
I saw thee as the new-blown blossoms fair,
Sprightly as light, and soft as summer's air;
Bright as their beams thy eyes a mind disclose,
While on thy lips gay blush'd the fragrant rose:
Wit, youth, and beauty, in each feature shone,
Press'd by my fate, I gaz'd—and was undone !
There died the generous fire, whose vigorous flame
Enlarg'd my soul, and urg'd me on to fame ;
Nor fame, nor wealth, my soften'd heart could move,
My heart, insensible to all but love 1
Snatch'd from myself my learning tasteless grew,
Vain my philosophy oppos'd to you.
A train of woes succeed, nor should we mourn
The hours which cannot, ought not to return.
As once to love I sway'd thy yielding mind,
Too fond, alas!—too fatally inclin'd!
To virtue now let me thy breast inspire,
And fen with zeal divine the holy fire ;
Teach thee to injur'd heaven, all-chang'd, to turn,
And bid thy soul with sacred raptures burn.
O that my own example could impart
This noble warmth to thy soft trembling heart!
That mine with pious undissembled care,
Might aid the latent virtue struggling there!
Alas I rave 1 nor grace, nor zeal divine,
Burns in a breast o'erwhelm'd with crimes like mine.
Too sure I find, while 1 the tortures prove
Of feeble piety, conflicting love,
On black despair my forc'd devotion built,
Absence, to me, has sharper pangs than guilt.
Ah! yet my Eloise, your charms I view,

Yet breathe my sighs, my tears yet pour for you;
Each weak resistance stronger knits my chain,
I sigh, weep, love, despair, repent—in vain,
Haste, Eloisa, haste, your Lover free,
Amidst your warmer prayers, O think of me!
Wing with your rising zeal my groveling mind,
And let me mine from your repentance find :
Ah! labor, strive, your love, yourself control,
The change will sure affect my kindred soul;
In blest consent our purer sighs shall grieve,
And heaven assisting shall our crimes forgive.
But if unhappy, wretched, lost, in vain,
Faintly th unequal combat you sustain ;
If not to Heaven you feel your bosom rise,
Nor tears refin'd fall contrite from your eyes ;
If still your heart its wonted passions move,
If still, to speak all pains in one—you love,
Deaf to the weak essays of living breath,
Attend the stronger eloquence of death.
When that kind Power this captive soul shall free,
(Which only then can cease to doat on thee)
When gently sunk to my eternal sleep,
The Paraclete my peaceful urn shall keep;
Then, Eloisa, then your Lover view,
See his quench'd eyes no longer fix'd on you;
From their dead orbs that tender utterance flown,
Which first to your's my heart's soft talc made known;
This breast no more (at length to ease consign'd)
Pant like the waving aspin in the wind;
See all my wild, tumultuous passions o'er,
And you, amazing change 1 belov'd no more;
Behold the destin'd end of human love—
But let the sight your zeal alone improve :

Let not your conscious soul, to sorrow mov'd,
Recal how much, how tenderly I lov'd;
With pious care your fruitless grief restrain,
Nor lesa tear your sacred veil profane;
Nor even a sigh on my cold urn bestow,
But let your breast with new-born raptures glow;
Let love divine frail mortal love dethrone,
And to your mind immortal joys make known;
Let Heaven relenting strike your ravish'd view,—-
And still the bright, the blest pursuit renew;
So with your crimes shall your misfortunes cease,
And your rack'd soul be calmly hush'd to peace.

EPISTLE XIII.

A BE LARD TO E LOIS A.

BY

JAMES CAfTTHORNE, M. A.

AH, why this boding start ? this sudden pain,
That wings my pulse, and shoots from vein to vein ?
What mean, regardless of yon midnight bell,
These earth-born visions saddening o'er my cell ?
What strange disorder prompts these thoughts to glow ?
These sighs to murmur, and these tears to flow ?
'Tis she, 'tis Eloisa's form rcstor'd,
Once a pure saint, and more than saints ador'd:
She comes in all her killing charms confest,
Glares thro' the gloom, and pours upon my breart.
Bid heaven's bright guard from Paraclete remove,
And drags me back to misery and love.

Enjoy thy triumphs, dear Illusion ! see
This sad apostate fronr his God to thee ;
Sec, at thy call, my guilty warmths return,
Flame thro' my blood, and steal me from my urn.
Yet, yet, frail Abelard! one effort try,
Ere the last lingering spark of virtue die;
The deadly charming sorceress control,
And spite of nature tear her from thy soul.

I Long has that soul in these unsocial woods,
Where anguish muses, and where horror broods,
From love's wild visionary wishes stray'd,
And sought to lose thy beauties in the shade,
Faith dropt a smile, devotion lent her fire,
Woke the keen pang, and sanctified desire;
Led me enraptur'd to the blest abode,
And taught my heart to glow with all its God.
But oh, how weak fair faith and virtue prove !
When Eloisa melts away in love!
When her fond soul impassioned, rapt, unveil'd,
No joy forgotten, and no wish conceai'd,
Flows thro' her pen as infant softness free,
And fiercely springs in ecstasies to me.
Ye heavens ! as walking in yon sacred fane—
With every seraph warm in every vein,
Just as remorse had rous'd an aking sigh,
And my torn soul hung trembling in my eye,
In that kind hour thy fatal letter came,
I saw, I gaz'd, I shiver'd at the name;
The conscious lamps at once forgot to shine,
Prophetic tremors shook the hallow'd shrine;
Priests, censers, altars from thy Genius fled,

And heaven itself shut on me while I read.

Dear smiling mischief! art thou still the same,
The still pale victim of too soft a flame?
Warm, as when first with more than mortal shine
Each melting eye-ball mix'd thy soul with mine?
Have not thy tears for ever taught to flow,
The glooms of absence, and the pangs of woe,
The pomp of sacrifice, the whisper'd tale,
The dreadful vow yet hovering o'er thy veil,
Drove this bewitching fondness from thy breast?
Curb'd the loose wish, and form'd each pulse to rest
And canst thou still, still bend the suppliant knee
To love's dead shrine, and weep and sigh for me?
Then take me, take me, lock me in thy arms,
Spring to my lips, and give me all thy charms:
No, fly me, fly me, spread th' impatient sail,
Steal the lark's wing, and mount the swiftest gale.
Skim the last ocean, freeze beneath the pole;
Renounce me, curse me, root me from thy soul;
Fly, fly, for justice bares the arm of God;
And the grasp'd vengeance only waits his nod.

Are these my wishes? can they thus aspire?
Does phrenzy form them, or does grace inspire?
Can Abelard, in hurricanes of zeal,
Betray his heayt, and teach thee not to feel?
Teach thy enamor'd spirit to disown
Each human warmth, and chill thee into stone?
Ah, rather let my tenderest accents move
The last wild tumults of unholy love!
On that dear bosom trembling let me lie,
Four out my soul, and in fierce raptures die,

Rouze all my passions, act my joys anew,
Farewell, ye cells I ye martyr'd saints ! adieu:
Sleep. conscience, sleep 1 each awful thought be drown'd,
And seven-fold darkness veil the scene around.
What means this pause, this agonizing start
This glimpse of heaven quick-rushing thro' my heart ?
Methinks I see a radiant cross display'd,
A wounded Saviour bleeds along the shade;
Around th' expiring God bright angels fly,
Swell the loud hymn, and open all the sky:
Q save me, save me, ere the thunders roll,
And hell's black caverns swallow up my soul.

Return, ye hours! when guiltless of a stain,
My strong-plum'd genius throb'd in every vein,
When warm'd with all th' Aegyptian fanes inspir'd,
All Athens boasted, and all Rome admir'd; .
My merit in its full meridian shone,
Each rival blushing, and each heart my own.
Return, ye scenes! ah no, from fancy fly,
On time's stretch'd wing, till each idea die,
Eternal fly, since all that learning gave
Too weak to conquer, and too fond to save,
To Love's soft empire every wish betray'd,
And left my laurels withering in the shade.
Let me forget, that while deceitful fame
Grasp'd her shrill trump, and fill'd it with my name,
Thy stronger charms, impower'd by Heaven to move
Each saint, each blest insensible to love,
At once my soul from bright ambition won,
I hugg'd the dart, I wish'd to be undone;
No more pale Science durst my thoughts engage,
Insipid dulness hung on every page;

The midnight lamp no more enjoy'd its blaze,
No more my spirits flew from maze to maze:
Thy glances bade Philosophy resign
Her throne to thee, and every sense was thine.

But what could all the frosts of wisdom do,
Oppos'd to beauty, when it melts in you?
Since these dark, chearless, solitary caves,
Death-breathing woods, and daily-opening graves,
Mis-shapen rocks, wild images of woe,
For ever howling to the deeps below;
Ungenial deserts, where no vernal shower
' Wakes the green herb, or paints th' unfolding flower;
Th' imbrowning glooms these holy mansions shed,
The night-born horrors brooding o'er my bed,
The dismal scenes black melancholy pours
O'er the sad visions of enanguish'd hours;
Lean abstinence, wan grief, low-thoughted care,
Distracting guilt, and hell's worst fiend, Despair,
Conspire, in vain, with all the aids of art,
To blot thy dear idea from my heart.

Delusive, sightless God of warm desire!
Why would'st thou wish to set a wretch on fire?
Why lives thy soft divinity where woe
Heaves the pale sigh, and anguish loves to glow?
Fly to the mead, the daisy-painted vale,

Breathe in its sweets, and melt along the gale;
Fly where gay scenes luxurious youths employ,
Where every moment steals the wing of joy:
There may'st thou see, low prostrate at thy throne,
Devoted slaves and victims all thy own:

Each village-swain the turf-built shrine shall raise,
And king's command whole hecatombs to blaze.

O memory 1 ingenious to revive
Each fleeting hour, and teach the past to live,
Witness what conflicts this frail bosom tore !
What griefs I suffer'd ! and what pangs I bore !
How long I struggled, labor'd, strove to save
An heart that panted to be still a slave!
When youth, warmth, rapture, spirit, love, and flame,
Seiz'd every sense, and burnt thro' all my frame;
From youth, warmth, rapture, to these wilds
I fled, My food the herbage, and the rock my bed.
There, while these venerable cloisters rise
O'er the bleak surge, and gain upon the skies,
My wounded soul indulg'd the tear to flow
O'er all her sad vicissitudes of woe ;
Profuse of life, and yet afraid to die,
Guilt in my heart, and horror in my eye,
With ceaseless prayers, the whole artillery given
To win the mercies of offended Heaven,
Each hill, made vocal, echoed all around,
While my torn breast knock'd bleeding on the ground.
Yet, yet, alas I tho' all my moments fly
Stain'd by a tear, and darkened in a sigh;
Tho' meagre fasts have on my cheek display'd
The dusk of death, and sunk me to a shade.
Spite of myself the still-impoisoning dart
Shoots thro' ray blood, and drinks up all my heart ;
My vows and wishes wildly disagree, .
And grace itself mistakes my God for thee.

Athwart the glooms, that wrap the midnight sky,

My Eloisa steals upon my eye; For ever rises in the solar ray,
A phantom brighter than the blaze of day:
Where-e'er I go, the visionary guest

Pants on my lip, or sinks upon my breast;
Unfolds her sweets, and, throbbing to destroy,
Winds round my heart in luxury of joy;
While loud hosannas shake the shrines around,
I hear her softer accents in the sound;
Her idol-beauties on each altar glare,
And Heaven much-injur'd has but half my prayer:
No tears can drive her hence, no pangs control,
For every object brings her to my soul.

Last night, reclining on yon airy steep,
My busy eyes hung brooding o'er the deep;
The breathless whirlwinds slept in every cave,
And the soft moon-beam danc'd from wave to wave;
Each former bliss in this bright mirror seen,
With all my glories, dawn'd upon the scene,
Recall'd the dear auspicious hour anew,
Whengrny fond soul to Eloisa flew:
When, with keen speechless ecstasies opprest,
Thy frantic lover snatch'd thee to his breast,
Gaz'd on thy blushes arm'd with every grace,
And saw the goddess beaming in thy face ;
Saw thy wild, trembling, ardent wishes move
Each pulse to rapture, and each glance to love.
But lo! the winds descend, the billows roar,
Foam to the clouds, and burst upon the shore,
Vast peals of thunder o'er the ocean roll,
The flame-wing'd lightning gleams from pole to pole.
At once the pleasing images withdrew,

And more than horrors crowded on my view;
Thy uncle's form, in all his ire array'd,
Serenely dreadful stalk'd along the shade,
Pierc'd by his sword, I sunk upon the ground,
The spectre ghastly smi'd upon the wound;
A group of black Infernals round me hung, .
And toss'd my infamy from tongue to tongue.

Detested Wretch 1 how impotent thy age!
How weak thy malice \ and how kind thy rage !
Spite of thyself, inhuman as thou art,
Thy murdering hand has left me all my heart;
Left me each tender, fond affection, warm,
A nerve to tremble, and an eye to charm.
Nocruel, cruel, exquisite in ill,
Thou thought'st it dull barbarity to kill;
My death had robb'd lost vengeance of her toil,
And scarcely warm'd a Scythian to a smile :
Sublimer Furies taught thy soul to glow
With all their savage mysteries of woe ;
Taught thy unfeeling poniard to destroy
The powers of nature, and the source of joy ;
To stretch me on the racks of vain desire,
Each passion throbbing, and each wish on fire;
Mad to enjoy, unable to be blest,
Fiends in my veins, and hell within my breast.
Aid me, fair Faith ! assist me, Grace divine!
Ye Martyrs ! bless me, and ye Saints! refine,
Ye sacred groves' ye heaven-devoted walls!
Where folly sickens, and where virtue calls;
Ye vows! ye altars! from this bosom tear
Voluptuous love, and leave no anguish there:
Oblivion! be thy blackest plume display'd

O'er all my griefs, and hide me in the shade;
And thou, too fondly idoliz'd ! attend,
While awful reason whispers in the friend;
Friend, did I say ? immortals ! what a name
Can dull, cold friendship, own so wild a flame
No; let thy Lover, whose enkindling eye
Shot all his soul between thee and the sky,
Whose warmths bewitch'd thee, whose unhallow'd song
Call'd thy rapt ear to die upon his tongue,
Now strongly rouze, while heaven his zeal inspires,
Diviner transports, and more holy fires;
Calm all thy passions, all thy peace restore,
And teach that snowy breast to heave no more.

Torn from the world, within dark cells immur'd,
By Angels guarded, and by vows secur'd,
To all that once awoke thy fondness dead,
And hope, pale sorrow's last sad refuge, fled;
Why wilt thou weep, and sigh, and melt in vain,
Brood o'er false joys, and hug th' ideal chain?
Say, canst thou wish, that, madly wild to fly
From yon bright portal opening in the sky,
Thy Abelard should bid his God adieu,
Pant at thy feet, and taste thy charms anew ?
Ye heavens! if, to this tender bosom woo'd
Thy meer idea harrows up my blood;
If one faint glimpse of Eloise can move
The fiercest, wildest agonies of love;
What shall I be, when, dazzling as the light,
Thy whole effulgence flows upon my sight ?
Look on thyself, consider who thou art,
And learn to be an Abbess in thy heart;
See, while devotion's ever-melting strain

Pours the loud organ thro' the trembling fane,
Yon pious Maids each earthly wish disown,
Kiss the dread cross, and crowd upon the throne:
O let thy soul the sacred charge attend,
Their warmths inspirit, and their virtues mend;
Teach every breast from every hymn to steal
The Seraph's meekness, and the Seraph's zea;
To rise to rapture, to dissolve away
In dreams of heaven, and lead thyself the way,
Till .ail the glories of the blest abode
Blaze on the scene, and every thought is God.
While thus thy exemplary cares prevail,
And make each vestal spotless as her veil,
Th' Eternal Spirit o'er thy cell shall move
In the soft image of the mystic dove;
The long-lost gleams of heavenly comfort bring,
Peace in his smile, and healing on his wing;
At once Temove affliction from thy breast,
Melt o'er thy soul, and hush her pangs to rest.

O that my soul, from love's curst bondage free,
Could catch the transports that I urge to thee!
O that some Angel's more than magic art
Would kindly tear the hermit from his heart!
Extinguish every guilty sense, and leave
No pulse to riot, and no sigh to heave.
Vain fruitless wish ! still, still, the vigorous flame
Bursts, like an earthquake, thro' my shatter'd frame;
Spite of the joys that Truth and Virtue prove,
1 feel but thee, and breathe not but to love;
Repent in vain, scarce wish to be forgiven ;
Thy form my idol, and thy charms my heaven.

Yet, yet, my Fair! thy nobler efforts try,
Lift me from earth, and give me to the sky;
Let my lost soul thy brighter virtues feel,
Warm'd with thy hopes, and wing'd with all thy zeal.
And when, low-bending at the hallow'd shrine,
Thy contrite heart shall Abelard resign;
When pitying heaven, impatient to forgive,
Unbars the gates of light, and bids thee live;
Seize on th' auspicious moment ere it flee,
And ask the same immortal boon for me.

Then when these black, terrific scenes are o'er,
And rebel nature chills the soul no more;
When on thy cheek th' expiring roses fade,
And thy last lustres darken in the shade;
When arm'd with quick varieties of pain,
Or creeping dully slow from vein to vein,
Pale Death shall set my kindred spirit free,
And these dead orbs forget to doat on thee;
Some pious friend, whose wild affections glow
Like ours, in sad similitude of woe,
Shall drop one tender, sympathizing tear,
Prepare the garland, and adorn the bier;
Our lifeless reliques in one tomb enshrine,
And teach thy genial dust to mix with mine.
Mean while, divinely purg'd from every stain,
Our active souls shall climb th' etherial plain,
To each bright Cherub's purity aspire,
Catch all his zeal, and pant with all his fire;
There, where no face the glooms of anguish wears,
No uncle murders, and no passion tears,
Enjoy with heaven eternity of rest,
For ever blessing, and for ever blest.

EPISTLE XIV.

THE
AFRICAN PRINCE,
NOW IN ENGLAND,

TO
ZARA
AT HIS FATHER'S COURT.

WRITTEN IN THE YEAR M DCCXLIX.
BY WILLIAM DODD, L. L. D.

PRINCES, my Fair, unfortunately great,
Born to the pompous vassalage of state,
Whene'er the Public calls, are doom'd to fly
Domestic bliss, and break the private tie,
Fame pays with empty breath the toils they bear,
And love's soft joys are chang'd for glorious care;
Yet conscious Virtue, in the silent hour,
Rewards the hero with a noble dower.
For this alone I dar'd the roaring sea,
Yet more, for this I dar'd to part with Thee.
But while my bosom feels the nobler flame,
Still unreprov'd, it owns thy gentler claim.
Though virtue's awful form my soul approves,
'Tis thine, thine only, Zara, that it loves.
A private lot had made the claim but one,
The Prince alone must love for virtue shun.
Ah! why, distinguish'd from the happier crowd,
To me the bliss of millions disallow'd ?
Why was I singled for imperial sway,

Since love and duty point a different way ?

Fix'd the dread voyage, and the day decreed,
When, duty's victim, love was doom'd to bleed,
Too well my mera'ry can these scenes renew,
We met to sigh, to weep our last adieu.
That conscious palm, beneath whose towering shade
So oft our vows of mutual love were made;
Where hope so oft anticipated joy,
And plann'd of future years the best employ;
That palm was witness to the tears we shed,
When that fond hope, and all those joys were fled.
Thy trembling lips, with trembling lips, I prest,
And held thee panting to my panting breast.
Our sorrow, grown too mighty to sustain,
Now snatch'd us, fainting, from the sense of pain.
Together sinking in the trance divine, —
I caught thy fleeting soul, and gave thee mine !
O ! blest oblivion of tormenting care !
O! why recall'd to life and to despair ?
The dreadful summons came, to part—and why ?
Why not the kinder summons but to die ?
To die together were to part no more,
To land in safety on some peaceful shore,
Where love's the business of immortal life,
And happy spirits only guess at strife.
" If in some distant land my prince should find
Some nymph more fair, you cry'd, as Zara kind"
Mysterious doubt! which could at once impart
Relief to mine, and anguish to. thy heart;
Still let me triumph in the fear exprest,
The voice of love that whisper'd in thy breast;
Nor call me cruel, for my truth shall prove

'Twas hut the vain anxiety of love,

Torn from thy fond embrace, the strand \ gain,
Where mourning friends inflict superfluous pain;
My Father there his struggling sighs supprest, .
And in dumb anguish clasp'd me to his breast,
Then sought, conceal'd the conflict of his mind,
To give the fortitude he could not find;
Eadh life-taught precept kindly he renew'd,
" Thy country's good, said he, be still pursu'd !
If, when the gracious gods my Son restore,
These eyes shall sleep in death, to wake no more;
If then these limbs, that now in age decay,
Shall mouldering mix with earth's parental clay;
Round my green tomb perform the sacred rite,
Assume my throne, and let thy yoke be light;
From lands of freedom glorious precepts bring,
And reign at once a father and a king."

How vainly proud, the arrogantly great
Presume to boast a monarch's godlike state !
Subject alike, the peasant and the king,
To life's dark ills, and care's corroding sting.
From guilt and fraud, that strikes in silence sure,
No shield can guard us, and no arms secure.
By these, my Fair, subdu'd, thy Prince was lost,
A naked captive on a barb'rous coast.

Nurtur'd in ease, a thousand servants round,
My wants prevented, and my wishes.crown'd,
No painful labors stretch'd the tedious day,
On downy feet my moments danc'd away.
Where-e'er I look'd, officious courtiers bow'd,

Where-e'er I pass'd, a shouting people crowd ;
No fears intruded on the joys I knew,
Each man my friend, my lovely mistress You.
What dreadful change! abandon'd and alone
The shouted prince is now a slave unknown:
To watch his eye no bending courtiers wait,
No hailing crowds proclaim his regal state ;
A slave condemn'd, with unrewarded toil,
To turn, from morn to eve, a burning soil,
Fainting beneath the sun's meridian heat,
Rouz'd by the scourge, the taunting jest I meet: "
Thanks to thy friends, they cry, whose care recalls
A prince to life, in whom a nation falls !"
Unwholesome scraps, my strength but half sustain'd,
From corners glean'd, and ev'n by dogs disdain'd;
At night I mingled with a wretched crew,
Who by long use with woe familiar grew;
Of manners brutish, merciless, and rude,
They mock'd my sufferings, and my pangs renew'd:
In groans, not sleep, I pass'd the weary night,
And rose to labor with the morning light.

Yet, thus of dignity and ease beguil'd,
Thus scorn'd and scourg'd, insulted and revil'd,
If Heaven with thee my faithful arms had blest,
And fili'd with love my intervals of rest,
Short though they were, my soul had never known
One secret wish to glitter on a throne;
The toolsome day had heard no sigh of mine,
Nor stripes, nor scorn, had urg'd me to repine.
A monarch, still beyond a monarch blest,
Thy love my diadem, my throne thy breast;
My courtiers, watchful of my looks, thy eyes,

Should shine, persuade, and flatter, and advise;
Thy voice my music, and thy arms should be
Ah! not the prison of a slave in me!
Could I with infamy content remain,
And wish thy lovely form to share my chain?
Could this bring ease, forgive th' unworthy thought,
And let the love that sinn'd atone the fault?
Could I, a slave, and hopeless to be free,
Crawl, tamely recent from the scourge, to thee?
Thy blooming beauties could these arms embrace?
My guilty joys enslave an infant race?
No: rather blast me, lightnings, whirlwind tear,
And drive these limbs in atoms through the air;
Rather than this, OI curse me still with life,
Ami let ray Zara smile a rival's wife:
Be mine alone th' accumulated woe,
Nor let me propagate my curse below.

But, from this dreadful scene, with joy I turn:
To trust in Heaven, of me let Zara learn.
The wretch, the sordid hypocrite, who sold
His charge, an unsuspecling prince, for gold,
That justice mark'd, whose eyes can never sleep,
And death commission'd, smote him on the deep.
The generous crew their port in safety gain,
And tell my mournful tale, nor tell in vain;
The king, with horror of th' atrocious deed,
In haste commanded, and the slave was freed.
No more Britannia's cheek, the blush of shame
Burns for my wrongs, her king restores her fame;
Propitious gales, to Freedom's happy shore
Waft me triumphant, and the Prince restore;
Whate'er is great and. gay around me shine,

And all the splendor of a court is mine.
Here knowledge too, by piety refin'd,
Sheds a bright radiance o'er my brightening mind;
From earth I travel upward to the sky,
I learn to live, to reign, yet more, to die.
I have' tales to tell, of love divine
Such blissful tidings! they shall soon be thine!
I long to tell thee, what, amaz'd, I see,
What habits, buildings, trades, and polity!
How art and nature vie to entertain
In public shows, and mix delight with pain
O! Zara, here, a story like my own,
With mimic skill, in borrow'd names, was shown;
An Indian chief, like me, by fraud betray'd,
And partner in his woes an Indian maid.
I can't recall the scenes, 'tis pain too great,
And, if recall'd, should shudder to relate.

To write the wonders here, I strive in vain;
Each word would ask a thousand to explain,
The time shall come, O! speed the lingering hour!
When Zara's charms shall lend description power
When, plac'd beside thee in the cool alcove,
Or through the green savannahs as we rove,
The frequent kiss shall interrupt the tale,
And looks shall speak my sense, though language fail.
Then shall the prodigies that round me rise
Fill thy dear bosom with a sweet surprise;
Then all my knowledge to thy faithful heart,
With danger gain'd, securely I'll impart.
Methinks I see thy changing looks express
Th' alternate sense of pleasure and distress;
As ail the windings of my fate I trace,

And wingthy fancy swift from place to place.
Yet where, alas! has flattering thoughts convey'd
The ravish'd Lover with his darling Maid?
Between us still unmeasur'd oceans roll,
Which hostile barks infest, and storms control.
Be calm, my bosom, since th' unmeasur'd main,
And hostile barks, and storms, are God's domain:
He rules resistless, and his power shall guide
My life in safety o'er the roaring tide;
Shall bless the love that's built on virtue's base,
And spare me to evangelize my race.
Farewell! thy Prince still lives, and still is free :
Farewell! hope all things, and remember Me.

EPISTLE XV.

ZARA,
AT THE COURT OF ANAMABOE.

TO THE
AFRICAN PRINCE,
WHEN IN ENGLAND.

By the Same.

SHOULD I the language of my heart conceal,
Nor warmly paint the passion that I feel;
My rising wish should groundless fears confine,
And doubts ungenerous chill the glowing line;
Would not my Prince, with nobler warmth, disdain
That love, as languid, which could stoop to feign?
Let guilt dissemble—in my faithful breast
Love reigns unblam'd, and be that love confest.

I give my bosom naked to thy view;
For what has shame with innocence to do?
In fancy now I clasp thee to my heart,
Exchange my vows, and all my joys impart.
I catch new transport from thy speaking eye;
But whence this sad involuntary sigh?
Why pants my bosom with intruding fears?
Why, from my eyes, distill unbidden tears?
Why do my hands thus tremble as I write?
Why fades thy lov'd idea from my sight?
O! art thou safe on Britain's happy shore,
From winds that bellow, and from seas that roar?
And has my Prince—(Oh, more than mortal pain!)
Betray'd by ruffians, felt the captive's chain?
Bound were those limbs, ordain'd alone to prove
The toils of empire, and the sweets of love?
Hold, hold! Barbarians of the fiercest kind!
Fear Heaven's red lightning—'tis a Prince ye bind;
A Prince, whom no indignities could hide,
They knew, presumptuous! and the Gods defy'd.
Where-e'er he moves, let love-join'd reverence rise,
And ail mankind behold with Zara's eyes!

Thy breast alone when bounding o'er the waves
To Freedom's climes, from slav'ry and from slaves;
Thy breast alone the pleasing thought could frame
Of what I felt, when thy dear letters came:
A thousand times 1 held them to my breast,
A thousand times my lips the paper prest:
My full heart panted with a joy too strong,
And ' Oh, my Prince 1' dy'd fauhering on my tongue;
Fainting, I sunk, unequal to the strife,
And milder joys sustain'd returning life.

Hope, sweet enchantress, round ray love sick head
Delightful scenes of blest delusion spread.

" COME, come, my Prince! my charmer ! haste away;
Come, come, I cry'd, thy Zara blames thy stay.
For thee the shrubs their richest sweets retain ;
For thee, new colors wait to-paint the plain ;
For thee, cool breezes linger in the grove,
The birds expec! thee in the green alcove;
Till thy return, the rills forget to fall,
Till thy return, the sun, the soul of all
He comes, my maids, in his meridian charms,
He comes refulgent to his Zara's arms;
With jocund songs proclaim my love's return ;
With jocund hearts his nuptial bed adorn.
Bright as the sun, yet gentle as the dove,
He comes, uniting majesty with love."—
Too soon, alas ! the blest delusion flies ;
Care swells my breast, and sorrow fills my eyes.
Ah! why do thy fond words suggest a fear—
Too vast, too numerous, those already here!
Ah I why with doubts torment my bleeding breast,
Of seas which storms control, and foes infest !
My heart, in all this tedious absence, knows
No thoughts but those of seas, and storms, and foes.

Each joyless morning, with the rising sun,
Quick the strand my feet spontaneous run :
" Where, where's ray Prince! what tidings have you brought ?"
Of each I met, with pleading tears I sought.
In vain I sought; some, conscious of my pain,
"With horrid silence pointed to the main.
Some with a sneer the brutal thought exprest,

And plung'd the dagger of a barb'rous jest:
Day follow'd day, and still I wish'd the next,
New hopes still flatter'd, and new doubts perplex'd;
Day follow'd day, the wish'd to-morrow came,
May hopes, doubts, fears, anxieties the same.
At length—" O Power Supreme! whoe'er tho art,
Thy shrine the sky, the sea, the earth, or heart;
Since every clime, and all th* unbounded main,
And hostile barks, and storms are thy domain,
If faithful passion can thy bounty move,
And Goodness sure must be the friend of love,
Safe to heese arms my lovely prince restore, safe to his
Zara's arms, to part no more.
 Oi grant prant to virtue thy protecting care,
And grant thy love to love's availing prayer;
Together then, and emulous to praise,
Aowery altar to thy name we'll raise;
There firs and last, on each returning day,
The our vows of gratitude we'll pay."

Fool that I was, to all my comfort blind,
Why, when thou went'st, did Zara stay behind
How could I fondly hope one joy to prove,
Midst all the wild anxieties of love?

Had fate in other mold thy Zara form'd,
And my bold breast in manly friendship warm'd,
How had I glow'd exulting at thy side!
How all the shafts of adverse fate defy'd
O yet a woman, and not nerv'd for toil,
With thee, OI had I turn'd a burning soil
In the cold prison had I lain with thee,
In love still happy, we had still been free;

Then fortune brav'd, had own'd superior might,
And pin'd with envy, while we fore'd delight.

Why should'st thou bid thy Love remember thee
Thine all my thoughts have been, and still shall be.
Each night the cool savannahs have I sought;
And breath'd the fondness of enamor'd thought;
The curling breezes mumur'd as I sigh'd,
And hoarse, at distance, roar'd my foe the tide :
My breast still haunted by a motley train,
Now doubts, now hopes prevail'd, now joy, now pain,
Now fix'd I stand, my spirit fled to thine,
Nor note the time, nor see the sun decline;
Now rquz'd I start, and wing'd with fear I run,
In vain, alas! for 'tis myself I shun.
When kindly sleep its lenient balm supply'd,
And gave that comfort waking thought deny'd.
Last night—but why, ah Zara! why impart,
The fond, fond fancies of a love-sick heart ?
Yet true delights on fancy's wings are brought,
And love's soft raptures realiz'd in thought—
Last night I saw, methinks I see it now—
Heaven's awful concave round thy Zara bow;
When sudden thence a flaming chariot flew,
Which earth received, and six white coursers drew.
Then—quick transition—did thy Zara ride,
Borne to the chariot—wond'rous—by thy side :
All glorious both, from clime to clime we flew,
Each happy clime with sweet surprize we view.
A thousand voices sung—" All bliss betide
The Prince of Libya, and his faithful bride!"
" 'Tis done, 'tis done," resounded through the skies,
And quick aloft the car began to rise;

Ten thousand beauties crowded on my sight,
Ten thousand glories beam'd a dazzling light.
My thoughts could bear no more, the vision fled,
And wretched Zara view'd her lonely bed.—
Come, sweet Interpreter, and ease my soul;
Come to my bosom, and explain the whole.
Alas! my Prince—yet hold, my struggling breast!
Sure we shall meet again, again be blest.
" Hope all, thou say'st, I live, and still am free ;"
O then prevent those hopes, and haste to me.
Ease all the doubts thy Zara's bosom knows,
And kindly stop the torrent of her woes.

But, that I know too well thy generous heart,
One doubt, than all, more torment would impart:
'Tis this; in Britain's happy courts to shine,
Amidst a thousand blooming maids, is thine
But thou, a thousand blooming maids among,
Art still thyself, incapable of wrong;
No outward charm can captivate thy mind,
Thy love is friendship heighten'd and refin'd;
'Tis what my soul, and not my form inspires,
And burns with spotless and immortal fires'.
Thy joys, like mine, from conscious truth arise,
And, known these joys, what others canst thou prize?
Be jealous doubts the curse of sordid minds:
Hence, jealous doubts, I give ye to the winds.—

Once more, O come! and snatch me to thy arms!
Come, shield my beating heart from vain alarms!
Come, let me hang enamor'd on thy breast,
Weep pleasing tears, and be with joy distrest!
Let me still hear, and still demand thy tale,

And, oft renew'd, still let my suit prevail!
Much still remains to tell and to enquire,
My hand still writes, and writing prompts desire;
My pen denies my last farewell to write,
Still, still " return," my wishful thoughts indite:
O! hear, my Prince, thy Love, thy Mistress call,
Think o'er each tender name, and hear by all.
O! pleasing intercourse of soul with soul,
Thus, while I write, I see, I clasp thee whole;
And these kind letters trembling Zara drew,
In every line shall bring her to thy view.
Return, return, in love and truth excell;
Return, I write; I scarce can add—Farewell.

EPISTLE XVI.

THE

DYING NEGRO.

@@@Kiiual P tar' aureus, attar n vtrrw rau,
IloXXotf tavXoK xVfjuxruf OV[J OS,
AxXavros, araQoq.@@@
EuRlPIDES.

ARM'D with thy sad last gift—the pow'r to die,
Thy shafts, stern Fortune, now I can defy;
Thy dreadful mercy points at length the shore,
Where all is peace, and men are slaves no more;
—This weapon, ev'n in chains, the brave can wield,
And vanquish'd, quit triumphantly the field: —
Beneath such wrongs let pallid Christians live,
Such they can perpetrate, and may forgive.

Yet while I tread that gulph's tremendous brink,
Where nature shudders, and where beings sink,
Ere yet this hand a life of torment close,
And end by one determin'd stroke my woes,
Is there a fond regret, which moves my mind
To pause and cast a ling'ring look behind ?
—O my lov'd bride!—for I have call'd thee min,
Dearer than life, whom I with life resign,
For thee ev'n here this faithful heart shall glow,
A pang shall rend me, and a tear shall flow.—
How shall I soothe thy grief, since fate denies
Thy pious duties to my closing eyes ?
I cannot clasp thee in a last embrace,
Nor gaze in silent anguish on thy face;
I cannot raise these fetter'd arms for thee,
To ask that mercy Heav'n denies to me;
Yet let thy tender breast my sorrows share,
Bleed for my wounds, and feel my deep despair.
Yet let thy tears bedew a wretch's grave,
Whom Fate forbade thy tenderness to save.
Receive these sighs—to thee my soul I breathe —
Fond love in dying groans is all I can bequeathed

Why did I, slave, beyond my lot aspire ?
Why didst thou fan the inauspicious fire ?
For thee I bade my drooping soul revive;
For thee alone I could have borne to live;
And love, I said, shall make me large amends,
For persecuting foes, and faithless friends :
Fool that I was 1 enur'd so long to pain,
Co trust to hope, or dream of joy again.
Joy, stranger guest, my easy faith betray'd,

And love now points to death's eternal shade
There while I rest from mis'ry's galling load,
Be thou the care of ev'ry pitying God !
Nor may that Daemon's unpropitious pow'r,
Who shed his influence on my natal hour,
Pursue thee too with unrelenting hate,
And blend with mine the color of thy fate.
For thee may those soft hours return again,
When pleasure led thee smiling o'er the plain,
Ere, like some hell-born spectre of dismay,
I cross'd thy path, and darken'd all the way.
Ye waving groves, which from this cell I view!
Ye meads now glitt'ring with the morning dew!
Ye flowers, which blush on yonder hated shore,
That at my baneful step shall fade no more,
A long farewell!—I ask no vernal bloom—
No pageant wreaths to wither on my tomb. —
Let serpents hiss and night-shade blacken there,
To mark the friendless victim of despair 1

And better in th' untimely grave to rot,
The world and all its cruelties forgot,
Than, dragg'd once more beyond the Western main,
To groan beneath some dastard planter's chain,
Where my poor countrymen in bondage wait
The slow enfranchisement of ling'ring fate.
Oh! my heart sinks, my dying eyes o'erflow,
When mem'ry paints the picture of their woe !
For I have seen them, ere the dawn of day,
Rouz'd by the lash, begin their chearless way;
Greeting with groans unwelcome morn's return,
Whne rage and shame their gloomy bosoms burn;
And, chiding ev'ry hour the slow-pac'd sun,

Endure their toils 'till all his race was run ;
No eye to mark their suff'rings with a tear,
No friend to comfort, and no hope to chear;
Then like the dull unpitied brutes repair
To stalls as wretched, and as coarse a fare;
Thank Heav'n one day of misery was o'er,
And sink to sleep, and wish to wake no more.—
Sleep'on I ye lost companions of my woes,
For whom in death this tear of pity flows ;
Sleep, and enjoy the only boon of Heav'n
To you in common with your tyrants giv'n !
O while soft slumber from their couches flies,
Still may the balmy blessing steep your eyes;
In sweet oblivion lull awhile your woes,
And brightest visions gladden the repose !
Let Fancy then, unconscious of the change,
Thro' our own fields, and native forests range ;
Waft ye to each once-haunted stream and grove,
And visit ev'ry.long lost scene ye love !
I sleep no more—nor in the midnight shade,
Invoke ideal phantoms to my aid;
Nor wake again, abandon'd and forlorn,
To find each dear delusion fled at morn ;
A slow-consuming death let others wait,
I snatch destruction from unwilling fate :—
Yon ruddy streaks the rising sun proclaim,
That never more shall beam upon my shame;
Bright orb ! for others let thy glory shine,
Mature the golden grain and purple vine,
While fetter'd Afric still for Europe toils,
And Nature's pl pund're rs riot on her spoils;
Be theirs the gifts thy partial rays supply,
Be mine the gloomy privilege to die.

And thou, whose impious avarice and pride
The holy Cross to my sad brows deny'd,
Forbade me Nature's common rights to claim,
Or share with thee a Christian's sacred name ;
Thou too farewell!—for not beyond the grave
Extends thy pow'r, nor is my dust thy slave.
In vain Heav'n spreads so wide the swelling sea,
Vast wat'ry barrier, 'twixt thy world and me;
Swift round the globe, by earth nor Heav'n control'd,
Fly stern oppression, and dire lust of gold.
Where-e'er the hell-hounds mark their bloody way,
Still nature groans, and man becomes their prey.
In the wild wastes of Afric's sandy plain,
Where roars the lion thro' his drear domain,
To curb the savage monarch in the chace,
There too Heav'n planted Man's majestic race ;
Bade Reason's sons with nobler titles rise,
Lift high Their brow sublime, and scan the skies.
What tho the sun in his meridian blaze
Dart on their naked limbs his scorching rays ?
What tho' no rosy tints adorn their face,
No silken tresses shine with flowing grace ?
Yet of ethereal temper are their souls,
And in their veins the tide of honor rolls;
And valor kindles there the hero's flame,
Contempt of death, and thirst of martial fame
And pity melts the sympathising breast,
Ah ! fatal virtue !—for the brave distrest.

My tortur'd bosom, sad remembrance spare!
Why dost thou plant thy keenest daggers there ?
And shew me what I was, and aggravate despair?

Ye streams of Gambia, and thou sacred shade !
Where in my youth's first dawn I joyful stray'd,
Oft have I rouz'd, amid your caverns dim,
The howling tyger, and the lion grim ;
In vain they gloried in their headlong force,
My javelin pierc'd them in their raging course.
But little did my boding mind bewray,
The victor and his hopes were doom'd a prey
To human brutes more fell, more cruel far than they.
Ah ! what avails the conqu'ror's bloody meed,
The gen'rous purpose, or the dauntless deed ? .
This hapless breast expos'd on ev'ry plain,
And liberty preferr'd to life in vain ?
Fall'n are my trophies, blasted is my fame,
Myself become a thing without a name,
The sport of haughty lords, and ev'n of slaves the shame.

Curst be the winds, and curst the tides which bore
These European robbers to our shore!
O be that hour involv'd in endless night,
When first their streamers met my wond'ring sight !
I call'd the warriors from the mountain's steep,
To meet these unknown terrors of the deep;
Rouz'd by my voice, their gen'rous bosoms glow,
They rush indignant, and demand the foe,
And poize the darts of death, and twang the bended bow:
When lo I advancing o'er the sea-beat plain,
I mark'd the leader of a warlike train.
Unlike his features to our swarthy race;
And golden hair play'd round his ruddy face.
While with insidious smile and lifted hand,
He thus accosts our unsuspecting band.
" Ye valiant chiefs, whom love of glory leads

To martial combats, and heroic deeds;
No fierce invader your retreat explores,
No hostile banner waves along your shores
From the dread tempests of the deep we fly,
Then lay, ye chiefs, these pointed terrors by:
And O, your hospitable cares extend,
So may ye never need the aid ye lend !
So may ye still repeat to ev'ry grove
The songs of freedom, and the strains of love !"
Soft as the accents of the traitor flow,
We melt with pity, and unbend the bow;
With lib'ral hand our choicest gifts we bring,
And point the wand'rers to the freshest spring.
Nine days we feasted on the Gambian strand,
And songs of friendship echo'd o'er the land.
When the tenth morn her rising lustre gave,
The chief approach 'd me by the sounding wave.
" O, Youth, he said, what gifts can we bestow
Or how requite the mighty debt we owe ?
For lo! propitious to our vows, the gale
With milder omens fills the swelling sail.
To-morrow's sun shall see our ships explore
These deeps, and quit your hospitable shore.
Yet while we linger, let us still employ
The number'd hours in friendship and in joy ;
Ascend our ships, their treasures are your own,
And taste the produce of a world unknown."

He spoke ; with fatal eagerness we burn,—.
And quit the shores, undestin'd to return !
The smiling traitors with insidious care,
The goblet proffer, and the feast prepare,
Till dark oblivion shades our closing eyes,

And ail disarmed each fainting warrior lies,
O wretches! to your future evils blind!
O morn for ever present to my mind!
When bursting from the treach'rous bands of sleep,
Rouz'd by the murmurs of the dashing deep,
I woke to bondage and ignoble pains,
And all the horrors of a life in chains.
Ye Gods of Afric I in that dreadful hour
Where were your thunders and avenging pow'r!
Did not my pray'rs, my groans, my tears invoke
Your slumb'ring justice to direct the stroke?
No pow'r descended to assist the brave,
No light'nings flash'd, and I became a slave.
From lord to lord my wretched carcase sold,
In Christian traffic, for their sordid gold:
Fate's blackest clouds were gather'd o'er my head;
And, bursting now, they mix me with the dead.

Yet when my Fortune cast my lot with Thine,
And bade beneath one roof our labors join,
Surpriz'd I felt the tumults of my breast
Lull'd by thy beauties to unwonted rest.
Delusive hopes my changing soul en flame,
And gentler transports agitate my frame.
What tho' obscure thy birth, superior grace
Shone in the glowing features of thy face.
Ne'er had my youth such winning softness seen,
Where Afric's sable beauties dance the green,
When some sweet maid receives her lover's vow,
And binds the offer'd chaplet to her brow.
While on thy languid eyes I fondly gaze,
And trembling meet the lustre of their rays,
Thou, gentle virgin, thou didst not despise

The humble homage of a captive's sighs.
By Heav'n abandon'd, and by man betray'd,
Each hope resign'd of comfort or of aid,
Thy gen'rous love could ev'ry sorrow end,
In thee I found a mistress and a friend;
Still as I told the story of my woes,
With heaving sighs thy lovely bosom rose;
The trickling drops of liquid crystal stole
Down thy fair cheek, and mark'd thy pitying soul:
Dear drops! upon my bleeding heart, like balm
They fell, and soon my tortur'd mind grew calm ;
Then my lov'd country, parents, friends forgot;
Heav'n I absolv'd, nor murmur'd at my lot;
Thy sacred smiles could ev'ry pang remove,
And liberty became less dear than love.

—And I have lov'd thee with as pure a fire,
As man e'er felt, or woman could inspire:
No pangs like these my pallid tyrants know,
Not such their transports, and not such their woe.
Their softer frames a feeble soul conceal,

A soul unus'd to pity or to feel;
Damp'd by base lucre, and repell'd by fear,
Each nobler passion faintly blazes here.
Not such the mortals burning Afric breeds,
Mother of virtues and heroic deeds!
Descended from yon radiant orb, they claim
Sublimer courage, and a fiercer flame. .
Nature has there, unchill'd by art, imprest
Her awful majesty on ev'ry breast.
Where'er she leads, impatient of control,
The dauntless Negro rushes to the goal;

Firm in his love, resistless in his hate,
His arm is conquest, and his frown is fate.

What fond affection in my bosom reigns
What soft emotions mingle with my pains !
Still as thy form before my mind appears,
My haggard eyes are bath'd in gushing tears;
Thy lov'd idea rushes to my heart,
And stern despair suspends the lifted dart
O could I burst these fetters which restrain
My struggling limbs, and waft thee o'er the main,
To some far distant shore, where Ocean roars
In horrid tempests round the gloomy shores;
To some wild mountain's solitary shade,
Where never European faith betray'd ;
How joyful could I, of thy love secure,
Meet ev'ry danger, ev'ry toil endure !
For thee I'd climb the rock, explore the flood,
And tame the famish'd savage of the wood;
When scorching summer drinks the shrinking streams,
My care should screen thee from its sultry beams;
At noon I'd crown thee with the fairest flowers,
At eve I'd lead thee to the safest bowers;
And when bleak winter howl'd around the cave,
For thee his horrors and his storms I'd brave;
Nor snows nor raging winds should damp my soul,
Nor such a night as shrowds the dusky pole;
O'er the dark waves my bounding skiff I'd guide,
To pierce each mightier monster of the tide ;
Thro' frozen forests force my dreadful way,
In their own dens to rouze the beasts of prey
Nor other blessing ask, if this might prove
How fix'd my passion, and how fond my love.

—Then should vain fortune to my sight display .
All that her anger now has snatch'd away;
Treasures more vast than Av' rice' erdesign'd
In midnight visions to a Christian's mind;
The Monarch's diadem, the Conqu'ror's meed,
That empty prize for which the valiant bleed
All that ambition strives to snatch from fete,
All that the Gods e'er lavish'd in their hate;
Not these should win thy lover from thy arms,
Or tempt a moment's absence from thy charms;
Indignant would I fly these guilty climes,
And scorn their glories as I hate their crimes !

But whither does my wand'ring fancy rove ?
Hence ye wild wishes of desponding love!
Ah I where is now that voice which lull'd my woes ?
That Angel-face, which sooth'd me to repose
By Nature tempted, and with passion blind,
Are these the joys Hope whisper'd to my mind ?
Is this the end of constancy like thine,
Are these the transports of a love like mine?
My hopes, my joys, are vanish'd into ai,
And now of ail that once engag'd my care,
These chains alone remain, this weapon and despair !

—So be thy life's gay prospects all o'ercast,
All thy fond hopes dire disappointment blast !
Thus end thy golden visions, son of pride!
Whose ruthless ruffians tore me from my bride;
That beauteous prize Heav'n had reserv'd at last,
Sweet recompence for all my sorrows past.
O may thy harden'd bosom never prove
The tender joys of friendship or of love

Yet may'st thou, doom'd to hopeless flames a prey,
In unrequited passion pine away!
May ev'ry transport violate thy rest,
Which tears the jealous lover's gloomy breast!
May secret anguish gnaw thy cruel heart,
'Till death in all his terrors wing the dart;
Then, to complete the horror of thy doom,
A favor'd rival smile upon thy tomb!

Why does my ling'ring soul her flight delay
Come, lovely Maid, and gild the dreary way!
Come, wildly rushing with disorder'd charms,
And clasp thy bleeding lover in thy arms;
Close his sad eyes, receive his parting breath,
And sooth him sinking to the shades of death!
O come—thy presence can my pangs beguile,
And bid th' inexorable tyrant smile;
Transported will I languish on thy breast,
And sink enraptur'd to eternal rest:
The hate of men, the wrongs of fate forgive,
Forget my woes, and almost wish to live.
Ah! rather fly, lest ought of doubt control
The dreadful purpose lab'ring in my soul;
Tears must not bend me, nor thy beauties move,
This hour I triumph over fate and love.
Again with tenfold rage my bosom burns,
And all the tempest of my soul returns;
Again the furies fire my madding brain,
And death extends his shelt'ring arms in vain;
For. unreveng'd I fall, unpity'd die;
And with my blood glut Pride's insatiate eye!

Thou Christian God! to whom so late I bow'd,

To whom my soul its new allegiance vow'd,
When crimes like these thy injur'd pow'r prophane,
O God of Nature! art thou call'd in vain?
Did'st thou for this sustain a mortal wound
While Heav'n, and Earth, and Hell, hung trembling round?
That these vile fetters might my body bind,
And agony like this distracl my mind?
On thee I call'd with reverential awe,
Ador'd thy wisdom, and embrac'd thy law;
Yet mark thy destin'd convert as he lies,
His groans of anguish, and his livid eyes,
These galling chains, polluted with his blood,
Then bid his tongue proclaim thee just and good 1
But if too weak thy vaunted power to spare,
Or suff'rings move thee not, O hear despair!
Thy hopes and blessings I alike resign,
But let revenge, let swift revenge be mine!
Be'this proud bark, which now triumphant rides,
Toss'd by the winds, and shatter'd by the tides!
And may these fiends, who now exulting view
The horrors of my fortune, feel them too!
Be theirs the torment of a ling'ring fate,
Slow as thy justice, dreadful as my hate;
Condemn'd to grasp the riven plank in vain,
And chac'd by all the monsters of the main;
And while they spread their sinking arms to thee,
Then let their fainting souls remember me!

—Thanks, righteous God!—Revenge shall yet be mine;
Yon flashing lightning gave the dreadful sign.
I see the flames of heav'nly anger hurl'd,
I hear your thunders shake a guilty world.
The time shall come, the fated hour is nigh,

When guiltless blood shall penetrate the sky.
Amid these horrors, and involving night,
Prophetic visions flash before my sight;
Eternal justice wakes, and in their turn
The vanquish'd triumph, and the victors mourn ;
Lo! Discord, fiercest of th' infernal band,
Fires all her snakes, and waves her flaming brand ;
No more proud Commerce courts the western gales,
But marks the lurid skies, and furls her sails;
War mounts his iron car, and at his wheels
In vain soft Pity weeps, and Mercy kneels;
He breathes a savage rage thro' all the host,
And stains with kindred blood the impious coast;
Then, while with horror sick'ning Nature groans,
And earth and heav'n the monstrous race disowns,—
Then the stern genius of my native land,
With delegated vengeance in his hand,
Shall raging cross the troubled seas, and pour
The plagues of Hell on yon devoted shore
What tides of ruin mark his ruthless way!
How shriek the fiends exulting o'er their prey !
I see their warriors gasping on the ground,
I hear their flaming cities crash around.—
In vain with trembling heart the coward turns,
In vain with.gen*rous rage the valiant burns.—
One common ruin, one promiscuous grave,
O'erwhelms the dastard, and receives the brave—
For Afric triumphs —his avenging rage
No tears can soften, and no blood assuage.
He smites the trembling waves, and at the shock
Their fleets are dash'd upon the pointed rock.
He waves his flaming dart, and o'er their plains
In mournful silence, desolation reigns—

Fly swift ye years!—Arise thou glorious morn!
Thou great avenger of thy race be born 1
The conqu'ror's palm and deathless fame be thine 1
One gen'rous stroke, and liberty be mine!
 And now, ye pow'rs! to whom the brave are dear,
Receive me falling, and your suppliant hear.
To you this unpolluted blood I pour,
To you that spirit which ye gave restore!
I ask no lazy pleasures to possess,
No long eternity of happiness;
But if unstain'd by voluntary guilt,
At your great call this being I have spilt,
For all the wrongs which innocent I share,
For ail I've suffer'd, and for all I dare ;
O lead me to that spot, that sacred shore,
Where souls are free, and men oppress no more

END OF EPISTLES HEROIC AND AMATORY.

NOTES ON EPISTLES
HEROIC AND AMATORY.

EPISTLE I.

Page.1 THE Author of this Epistle was of Sidney College,
Cambridge; and died at an early period, after having given various proofs of uncommon talents.

In 1728 was published a posthumous volume of his Poems.

EPISTLE III.

Page 16. The Duke of Suffolk, being at the instance of the Commons banished the realm, embarked for France, but was taken in his passage by a pirate, who, bringing him back to the English coast, beheaded him. Before his death, he is supposed to-write the following lines to his paramour Queen Margaret. The incidents are chiefly taken from the. first and second parts of Shakspere's historical plays of Henry the VIth.

21. Here must 1 fall, fast by the rolling main (Nor was the mutter'd spell pronounc'd in vain,)

Bol. Tell me what fates await the Duke of Suffolk?

Sp. By water shall he die, &c.
See Shakspere, 2d Part of Henry VI. A. 1. S. 3.

22. Of lordships wide and princely treasures vain,
The Benedicline rears his stately fane :] Marmoutier, a noble convent of Benedictines of the regulation of St. Maur. This magnificent structure stands about half a league from Tours, on the banks of the river Loire, by the side of the cliff which skirts the river almost from Blois to Tours, and its lofty-spire rises above the height of the rock. Amongst numerous treasures, it boasts the relics of St. Martin the patron Saint of Tours, and a ring of our Henry the Second, to whom Touraine, and most of the adjoining provinces which are watered by the Loire, belonged. The abbacy of this convent is annexed to the Archbishopric of Tours; the declivities of the rock, adjoining to this fabric, are famous for producing many excellent wines, the chief of which are exported at Bourdeaux. J.

24. But now, alas! far other thoughts arise,
Far other scenes distract my closing eyes!
For, ah! — An excellent letter of this unfortunate nobleman to his son, just before his own death, and many other interesting anecdotes respecting him, are preserved in the very curious collection of the Paston Letters, lately published by Sir John Fenn.—One, which relates, the particulars of his murder, is here

subjoined:

" To ike ryght worchipfull John Paston, at Norwich.

".Ryght worchipfull Sr. I recomaunde me to yow, and am right sory of that I shalle sey and have S0o weshe this litel bill with sorwfulle terys that on ethes (scarcely) ye shalle reede it.

" As on Monday nezte after May (day 4th. *May*) ther come tydyngs to London that on Thorsday before (30th of *April*) the Duke of Suff' come unto the costes of Kent full nere Dower with his ij shepes and a litel Spynn the qweche Spynn he sente with cteyn Lett's to cteyn of his trustid men unto Caleys warde to knowe howe he shuld be resceyvyd, and with hym mette a shippe callyd Nicolas of the Towre, with other shippis waytyng on hym, and by hem that were in the Spyner the maister of the Nicolas hadde knowlich of the Dukes amyng, and whanne he espyed the Dukes shepis he sent forth his bote to wete what they were, and the Duke hym selfe spakke to hem, and seyd he was be the Kyngs comaundement sent to Caleys ward,

" And they seyd he moste speke with here mast'and soo he wt ij or iij of his men wente forth wyth hem yn here bote to the Nicolas, and whanne he come the mast badde hym welcome Traito as me sey, and for th the maist desyryd to wete yf the Shepmen woldde holde with the Duke, and they sent word the wold not ynn noo wyse, and soo he was yn the Nicolas tyl Sa-tday next (2d. *May*) folwyng.

" Soom sey he wrotte moche thenke to be delyu 'd to the Kynge, but that is not verily knowe, he hadde his Confesso - with him, &c.

" And some sey he was arreyned yn the sheppe on here man upon the appechementes, and fonde gylty, &c.

" Also he asked the name of the sheppe, and whanne he knew it he remembred

Stacy that seid if he myght eschape the daung of the Towr he shud be saffe, and than his herte faylyd hym for he thowght he was dyssevyd, and yn the syght of all drawyn ought of the grete Shippe yn to the Bote, and there was an Exe and a stoke and oon of the lewdeste (meanest) of the shippe badde hym ley down hys hedde and he shud be fair ferd wyth and dye on a swerd, and smotte of his hedde withyn halfe a doseyn strokes, and toke awey his Gown of russette and his Dobelette of velvet mayled, and leyde his body on the Sonds of Dover, and some sey his hedde was sette oon a pole by it, and hes men sette on the londe grette circost nce and prey [*that is*, as 1 understand it, after the most circumstancial proofs of their not being accessories with the Duke, and intreaties to be discharged] and the Shreve of Kent doth weche the body and sent his Under Shreve to the Juges to wete what to doo, and also to the Kenge whatte shalbe doo. . " Fort her I wotte notte but this fer is y yf the p's (process) be erroneo lete his concell reu se it," &c.

This letter was written on Tuesday 5 of May 1450,, & in the 28 of Henry VI.

Sir John adds, that " the Duke's body was taken from Dover Sands, and carried to the Collegiate Church of Wingfield in Suffolk, where it lies interred under an altar tomb, in the Chancel, with his effigies in armor, painted, gilt, &c. carved in wood, lying on it. It is remarkably well executed, as is that of Alice his wife likewise, which lies at his right hand.

See Sir John Fenn's observations on the preceding narrative, in the ***Collection of the Pas ton Letters.***

EPISTLE IV.

Page 26. The Princess Mary, Henry the Eighth's younger sister, being in love with the Duke of Suffolk, was, for public reasons, married to Lewis the Twelfth of France, who died in six months after. The Queen, again at liberty, is supposed to write this Epistle to the Duke of Suffolk, her first lover.

EPISTLE V.

Page 32. To this Epistle the following Dedication was originally prefixed:

To the right honorable MARY LEPEL, Baroness" -Dowager Hervey of Ickworth, distinguished by her superior accomplishments, as the admirer and protectress of every elegant art, this Poem is, with the greatest respeft, inscribed, by her ladyship's obliged tumble servant,   GEORGE KEATE'.

Lady Jane Gray hath ever been regarded, as one of the most amiable and perfect characters, that the Records of any Nation have delivered down to Posterity. The Circumstances of her life are uncommon, if not unexampled, and her misfortunes as singular, as was the fortitude with which she sustained them; all conspiring to render her a fit subject for this species of Heroic Poetry, of which we have but few pieces in our language; though it seems to have a peculiar advantage of conveying, in the happiest manner, the sentiments of such Characters as are worthy of being celebrated.

The variety of accomplishments, which this unfor-tunate Princess crowded into the short period of ae-venteen years, and above all, that justness of thinking which she attained in so early an age, have deservedly gained her the admiration of succeeding times.

But her story is so well known, that it would be impertinence to dwell upon it.—Wedded to a Man she loved, and whose youth and virtues made him worthy of her affection, called to a crown against her will, throned and dethroned within the little compass of a fortnight, dragged from her palace to her prison, separated from a husband doomed to death, and sentenced to lose her own head on a scaffold;—Such were the distresses that surrounded her, when I ventured to put the pen into her hand: awake as she was to every passion and delicacy of sentiment, which LoVe, Disappointment, and Calamity could give birth to; yet, by the force of Religion, subduing their poignancy, and at last totally triumphing over them.

I much doubt whether I may have done sufficient justice to the character of this virtuous Lady; but hope at least, that I have not departed from Nature, in any Sentiment which I have attributed to her.

EPISTLE VI.

Page 46. Mr. Canning, the Author of this Epistle, was of the Middle Temple, and died April 11, 1771.

This Epistle is supposed to have been written by Lord Russel, on Friday night, July so, 1683, in New-gate; that prison having been the place of his con finement for some days immediately preceding his execution.

49. *Press'd by my Friends, and Rachel' fond desires,*] Lady Rachel Russel, his wife. See for various particulars relative to this respectable victim, the letters of that lady

50. *Let impious Escrick act such treacherous scenes,*] The perjuries of this noble Miscreant, against Lord Russel and Algernon Sydney, have branded his name with eternal infamy.

55. *of right divine let foolish FILM ER dream,"*] Sir Robert, author of the Patriarcha, &c, in support of arbitrary power, which the delirium of the times only could have rendered objects of confutation to SYD-NEY, LOCKE, and HOADLY.

60. *Let princely Monmouth courtly wiles Beware,*
Nor trust too far to fond paternal care;] James, Duke of Monmouth, son of Charles II. was concerned in the plot for which Lord Russel suffered, but for that turn escaped.

EPISTLE VII.

Page 63. When Marius was expell'd from Rome by Sylla's faction, and retired into Africa, his son (who accompanied him) fell into the hands of Hiemp sal king of Numidia, who kept him prisoner. One of the Mistresses of that king fell in love with Ma rius the younger, and was so generous to contrive and give him his liberty, though by that means she sacrificed her love for ever. It was after he had rejoined his father, that she is supposed to write. The substance of this Epistle is taken from **Fontenelle.**

EPISTLE Vill.

Page 69. Pompey, when he was very young, fell in love with Flora, a Roman courtezan, who was so very beautiful that the Romans had her painted to adorn the temple of Castor and Pollux. Geminius (Pompey's friend) afterwards fell in love with her also; but she, prepossessed with a passion for Pompey, would not listen to Geminius. Pompey, in compassion to his friend, yielded him his mistress, which Flora took so much to heart, that she fell dangerously ill; and in that sickness is supposed to write the foregoing letter to Pompey.

EPISTLE IX.

Page 74. Roxana, one of Usbeck's wives, was found (whilst he was in Europe) in bed with her lover, whom she had privately let in to the seraglio The guardian eunuch, who discovered them, had the man murdered on the spot, and her close guarded till he received instructions from his Master how to dispose of her. During that interval she swallowed poison, and is supposed to write this letter whilst she is dying. The substance of the Epistle will be found in **Les Lettres Persannes.**

EPISTLE X.

Page- 79. This Epistle, which Mr. Walpole pro-nounces the best of Lord Hervey's poetical productions, was designed as an address to the honorable Antony Lowther, from Miss Sophia Howe, Maid of 'Honor.

EPISTLE XII.

Page 97. Abelard and Eloisa flourished in the twelfth century: they were two of the most distinguished persons of their age in learning and beauty, but for nothing more famous than for their unfortunate passion. After a long course of calamities, they retired each to a several convent, and consecrated the remainder of their days to religion. It was many years after this separation, that a letter of Abelard's to a friend, which contained the history of his misfortunes, fell into the hands of Eloisa: this occasioned those celebrated letters (out of which the following is partly extracted), which gives so lively a picture of the struggles of grace and nature, virtue and passion. POPE.

The editor of Poems by eminent ladies in two vols. 12mo. printed for R. Baldwin in 1755, have ascribed this poem to Mrs. Madan, and paid her handsome compliments upon it; whereas Mr. Pattison was un-doubtedly the author. In the memoirs of his life prefixed to his poems, there is a letter dated York, Oft. 20, 1726, wherein this poem is mentioned as Pattison's, and much commended.

EPISTLE XIII.

Page 104. Mr. Cawthorne, born in the year 1720, at Sheffield in Yorkshire, was admitted of Clare-Hall, Cambridge, where he took his master's degree, and having received orders, became school-assistant in London to a Mr. Clare, whose Sister he afterward married. In the year 1760, he was killed by a fall from his horse, not long after his appointment by the skinner's Company to the

School at Tunbridge, over which he presided with ability equal to his harshness. Two Sermons and this Epistle were published by him, and since his death a collection of his Poems.

To the original publication of ABELARD to ELOISA *he* following verses were annexed.

TO
MISS—
OF HORSEMANDEN, IN KENT.

WHEN Wit and Science trim'd their withered bays
At Petrarch's vice, and beam'd with half their rays,
Some heav'n-born genius, panting to explore
The scenes Oblivion wish'd to live no more,
Found Abelard in grief's sad pomp array'd,
And call'd the melting mourner from the shade.
Touch'd by his woes, and kindling at his rage,
Admiring nations glow'd from age to age;
From age to age the soft infection ran,
Taught to lament the hermit in the man!
Pride dropt her crest, Ambition learn'd to sigh,
And dove-like Pity streamed in every eye.

Sick of the world's applause, yet fond to warm
Each maid that knows with Eloise to charm,
He asks of verse to aid his native fire,
Refines, and wildly lives along the lyre;
Bids all his various passions throb anew,
And hopes, my Fair, to steal a tear from you.
O blest with temper, blest with skill to pour
Life's every comfort on each social hour!
Chaste as thy blushes, gentle as thy mien,

Too grave for folly, and too gay for spleen
Indulg'd to win, to soften, to inspire,
To melt with music, and with wit to fire ;
To blend, as judgment tells thee how to please,
Wisdom with smites, and majesty with ease ;
Alike to virtue as the graces known,
And proud to love all merit but thy own !

These are thy honors, these will charms supply,
When those dear suns shall set in either eye !
While she, who, fond of dress, of paint and place,
Aims but to be a goddess in the face;
Born all thy sex illumines to despise,
Too mad for thought, too pretty to be wise,
Haunts for a year fantastically vain,
With half our Fribbles dying in her train ;
Then sinks, as beauty fades and passion cools,
The scorn of coxcombs, and the jest of fools

EPISTLE XIV.

Page 117. " This Epistle and the following were occasioned by the appearance in England of two Africans who had been trepanned by the captain of a trading vessel, and sold for slaves. One of them was a prince, intrusted to the wretch who betrayed him. A representation of their case by some of the crew to government, occasioned their being ransomed, and afterwards maintained, educated, and sent home to their own country, in a manner suitable to their births and stations. The Author, eldest son of a worthy clergyman, vicar of Bourne in Lincolnshire, was born May 29, 1729 ; and sent at the age of sixteen to the University of Cambridge, where he was admitted sizer of Clare-Hall. In 1750 he took his batchelor's degree with great reputation, in 1758 his master's, "and in 1766, that of doctor of laws. Having married and taken orders, on the foundation of the Magdalene Hospital he was appointed preacher; in 1763 he obtained from Bishop Squire, the prebend of Brecon; jn 1765 was nominated one of the King's chaplains, and was afterwards presented to Hocliffe in Bedfordshire. Indulging himself in a profligate extravagance beyond what his income would support, he was weak enough to write an anonymous letter to the Lady of Earl Bathurst who was at that time Chancellor, offering a sum of money, if through her in-terest he might be promoted to St. George's, Hanover Square. The discovery of this folly hastened his ruid. He was struck off the list of King's chaplains in consequence, and as his extravagance knew no limits, he was prompted to forge a bond from the Earl of Chesterfield, for which he was tried at the 014 Bailey, and being fully convicted, was executed at Tyburn, June 27, 1777."

123. *O! Zara, here, a story like my own,*
With mimic skill, in borrow'd names, was shown;]

An allusion to the play of Oroonoko, at which he was present, and so affected as to be unable to stay out its performance.

EPISTLE XVI.

Page 133. This Epistle was occasioned by a fact which had recently happened at the time of its first publication in 1773. A Negro, belonging to the Captain of a West-Indiaman, having agreed to marry a white woman, his fellow-servant, in order to effect: his purpose, had left his master's house, and procured himself to be baptized; but being detected and taken he was sent on board the Captain's vessel then lying in the River; where, finding no chance of escaping, and preferring death to the West-Indies, he took an opportunity of shooting himself. As soon as his de-termination is fixed, he is supposed to write this Epistle to his intended Wife.

To this Epistle the following **Dedication** was prefixed :

Having been, through indignation betrayed into the dangerous character of an Author, I sought among the professed philosophers of the eighteenth century, one whose name I might consistently prefix to an assertion of the rights of nature, and who would not blush at the homage of an unknown and unambitious bard. But I found that modern Philosophy herself participated of the refinement of modern manners : she has forgotten that she once inhabited the lowly cot of Socrates, and shared the frugal meals of Epaminondas; she no longer numbers in her train Senators and Generals, who descending from seats of magistracy, or cars of triumph, did not disdain to cultivate with their victorious arms that earth which they had defended with their blood. Her votaries are not now those stubborn souls who defied the tyrant on his throne, or in his death vindicated the rights of their country and of mankind. Nor are the rugged manners of Cato and Brutus, now formidable to usurpers; nor do the harsh principles of Diogenes suffuse a momentary blush upon the cheek of monarchy. Modern Philosophy, like modern Honor, has chosen her residence in' courts and palaces. There we find her favored votaries prostrate at the foot of thrones, and kissing the sacred dust. If she speak, it is to join her whispers to the thunders of prerogative, and to teach the subject world, that neither the will of Heaven, nor of Heaven-descended Kings, must be opposed.

Little qualified to sacrifice at the altars of this new divinity, I dared not implore the patronage of its ministers and priests ; still less did I find myself dis-posed to invoke those literati of the Continent, who are enemies to princes, yet stoop to flatter their minions and sycophants; moralists, yet men of pleasure; philosophers, yet foes to natural religion ; sceptics yet dogmatical; and who, while they profess disinte-restedness and independence, lead the venal muses to voluntary prostitution. Yet I found one man, whose matchless eloquence is less admirable than the fortitude with which he has developed the principles, and defended the rights of human nature; whose virtue is as unequalled as his genius; and whose life is a nobler pattern of imitation than his writings; who, rejecting the supercilious bounty of the vain, yet un pitying and ungenerous, Great; exerts a painful industry amidst the .evils and infirmities of old age, and prefers exile, poverty, and obscurity, to all the riches and the honors which ambitious meanness extorts from]Kings.—After this portrait is it necessary to subscribe a name, and to acknowledge, that 1 dedicate this poem

TO
JEAN JAQUES ROUSSEAU ?

It is probable that this tribute to your virtues may never reach your ears, and that the following lines, like the occasion of them, will soon be consigned to oblivion. Yet on this first, and probably last occa sion, in which I shall obtrude my sentiments upon the world, I may be excused, if I inscribe a piece, whose only merit is the humanity and freedom of its sentiments, to that Man, from whose writings I have principally derived them. Happy should I esteem myself could these feeble efforts once more awaken that irresistible eloquence, which was never prostituted to falshood, or denied to truth ; those talents of reasoning and investigation, which can never fail to convince the mind, that is not debased by voluntary and incorrigible error; and that virtuous enthusiasm which seems inspired by Heaven itself for the in? struction of its creatures. How should I rejoice tQ see a cause like this rescued from my weak pen ; tQ see the rights of humanity vindicated by him, who most intimately feels their force, and is most capable of expressing what he feels; to see that insolence, that successful avarice confounded, which, under the mask of commerce, has already ravaged the two extremir lies of the globe!—Astonish and instruc! posterity by the dreadful spectacle of human crimes; and while you represent in one quarter of the world a band of insatiable wretches, spreading unprovoked desolation over its most beautiful regions; massacring the Bramin in the midst of his uncontaminated feasts, and staining with blood the purest altars of the Deity; let the other exhibit a race of Christian merchants, daily trafficking for hecatombs of their fellow-.creatures in a lot; exhausting *Africa* to supply with slayes the countries they have depopulated in *America;*[1] and annually reducing millions to a state of -misery still more dreadful than death itself.—Should there be room for scenes less striking,,though equally instructive and important, let your enchanting pencil

> [1] In the single island of Jamaica above 60,000 of the natives are computed to have been cruelly exterminated by the first European settlers there.

exhibit a nation renowned for arts and arms; let the surrounding ocean be covered with her fleets ; and let her boast an inflexible sternness, and an unconquerable valor. Paint a savage and gloomy liberty exulting amidst the shock of foreign invasions and domestic tumults: let her wield a bloody axe, and trample alike on the mitre and the diadem: let superstition and civil war conspire to exalt her, until she have triumphed over opposition, and erected a temple, whose foundations appear durable, as the world itself. Beneath a milder sky let peace introduce the genius and arts which adorned the states of Athens and of Rome, without insuring their duration: let gentler manners, and a less ferocious dignity succeed ; let philosophy and science glory in a race of illustrious disciples, whose labors may dispel the gloom of fanaticism, and teach mankind whatever the Almighty has permitted them to know.—Here, while the delighted eye of presumption gazes with rapture, and pronounces the tablet perfect and eternal,—reverse the scene, and inscribe the motifying lesson of human imbecility. Introduce commerce and prosperity spreading over the land, and enervating the minds of men with a secret, but swift infection. Let avarice and sensuality succeed to honor; faction and servitude invade the asylum of liberty ; and manly reason, like a fettered lion, be dragged in triumph by fashion and caprice.—Such are the scenes I would present to my Countrymen, could I boast an eloquence like your's, to explain the eternal principles which Providence has decreed, shall influence the fate of nations ; the causes which exalt them to security and dominion, or plunge them into that abyss of baseness and corruption, whence they can no more emerge: such are the lessons for which you have been proscribed and persecuted by a world which you have enlightened. Yet has not the ingratitude of mankind ever tainted your philanthropy. You have taught us, that the sublime maxims of philosophy are not always confined to indolent speculation; you have shewn that a stoical severity is not always inconsistent with a feeling heart; and that the simplicity of ignorance is compatible with the most exalted genius[2].

The trifle now inscribed with your name, was oc-casioned by a particular fa ft ; but to the disgrace of human nature, the subjelt is sufficiently general to interest every heart not totally impenetrable. We boast of the gentleness of our manners, and think the rugged virtues of antiquity ill-adapted to the genius of the present times. When you ask if Brutus sold

[2] For though I fly to scape from Fortune's rage,

And bear the scars of envy, spite, and scorn,

Yet with mankind no horrid war I wage,

Yet with no impious spleen my breast is torn:

For virtue lost, and ruin'd man, I mourn.

BlATTIE..

his country, or the Spartan matrons frequented as emblies of nocturnal riot, it is thought a sufficient answer to say, that we do not expose our children, or whip them at the altar of Diana ; and that this is ths age of generous sentiment, and refined humanity. I will not compare the education of an ancient Spartan with that of a British nobleman. Let eunuchs and figurants, those respectable guardians of modern dis cipline, insult the memory of Lycurgus; and fellows; of colleges establish their monkish institutions on the ruin of the Lyceum. Let the present age enjoy the boldest panegyrics its admirers can bestow. But if our boasted improvements, and frivolous politeness, be well acquired by the loss of manly firmness and independence, if in order to feel as men it be necessary to adopt the manners of women, let us at least be consistent, nor mingle the excesses of barbarism with the weaknesses of civilization. There are certain forms in which vice appears not only monstrous, but ridiculous; the cruelty of Nero is more disgusting than that of Tiberius. When a benevolent mind contemplates the republic of Lygurgus, its admiration is mixed with a degree of horror. We behold a band of determined patriots, irresistible in war, and inflexible in peace; souls to which the severity of virtue was more engaging than its enjoyments; and who seemed to court the dangers of combat, only that they might refuse the rewards of viclory. Yet this admirable republic is tainted by atrocities, which tar nish the lustre of its sublime institutions. When we reflect that to form a small society of heroes, a much greater number of men sunk below the rank of brutes; when we consider the unfortunate *Heloses*, abused, insulted, and enslaved; we less admire the exaltation of one part of our species, than we execrate the degradation of another; heroism becomes displeasing at such a price, and we prefer the calm of jnediocrity to the terrors of so stormy an excellence. But let us not too hastily triumph in the shame of Sparta, lest we aggravate our own condemnation; Let us remember, there is a people who share the government and name of Britons; among whom the cruelty of Sparta is renewed without its virtue. It was some excuse for the disciples of Lycurgus, that if one man had been created by Heaven to obey ano ther, the citizens he had formed best deserved the empire of the world. But what has *America* to boast ? What are the graces or the virtues which distinguish lits inhabitants ? What are *their* triumphs in war, or their inventions in peace ? Inglorious soldiers, yet seditious citizens; sordid merchants, and indolent usurpers; behold the men, whose avarice has been more fatal to the interests of humanity, and has more . desolated the world than the ambition of its ancient Conquerors! For them the Negro is dragged from his cottage, and his plantane shade ;[3]—by them the

[3] These observations are by no means to be confined to the West Indies. " The number of Negroes in the Southern Colonies of North America is equal, if not superior, to that of the white men.—Their condition is truly pitiable 5 their labor excessively hard, their diet poor and scanty, their treatment cruel and oppressive. They cannot but be a subject of terror to those who so inhumanly tyrannize over them."

BURNABY'S Travels through North America in 1760.

fury of African tyrants is stimulated by pernicious gold; the rights of nature are invaded; and European faith becomes infamous throughout the globe. Yet, such is the inconsistency of mankind 1 these are the men whose clamours for liberty and independence are heard across the Atlantic Ocean! Murmurings and rebellions are the first fruits of their gratitude, and thus America recompences Europe for the protection she has bestowed.—But are the hopes and for-tunes of the species indeed fallen so low, that freedom will desert that country, whose warriors and philosophers have so often conspired to defend her, to seek an asylum in the forests of America ?—Much as an impartial observer may find to blame in Britain, her colonies, I fear, are not more acceptable to Providence.—Let the wild inconsistent claims of America prevail, when they shall be unmixed with the clank of chains, and the groans of anguish. Let her aim a dagger at the breast of her milder parent, if she can advance a step without trampling on the dead and dying carcasses of her slaves:—But let her remember; it is in Britain alone, that laws are equally favorable to liberty and humanity; it is in Britain that the sacred of nature have received their most awful ration.—Could I flatter myself that I might contri-to such a cause, or interest the generous minds ' Countrymen to extend an ampler protection to ost innocent and miserable of their own species, uld congratulate myself that I had not lived in —For the rest, I trust, that the motive of the r will, in your eyes, atone for his defects, and ou will allow him the only merit he assumes, and sincerity, when he subscribes himself a to human nature; and, consequently,

Tour FRIEND *and* ADMIRER.

ELEGIES

MORAL, DESCRIPTIVE, AND AMATORY.

ELEGY I.

BY WILLIAM WHITEHEAD, ESQ.

WRITTEN AT THE
CONVENT OF HAUT VILLIERS,
In Champagne, 1754.

SILENT and clear, through yonder peaceful vale,
While Marne's slow waters weave their mazy way,
See, to th' exulting sun, and fost'ring gale,

What boundless treasures his rich hanks display!

Fast by the stream, and at the mountain's base,
The lowing herds through living pastures rove:
Wide-waving harvests crown the rising space:
And still superior nods the viny grove,

High on the top, as guardian of the scene,
Imperial Sylvan spreads his umbrage wide;
Nor wants there many a cot, and spire between,
Or in the vale, or on the mountain's side,

To mark that man, as tenant of the whole,
Claims the just tribute of his culturing care,
Yet pays to Heaven, in gratitude of soul,
The boon which Heaven accepts.of, praise and prayer.

O dire effeth of war! the time has been
When Desolation vaunted here her reign ;
One ravag'd desart was yon beauteous scene,
And Marne ran purple to the frighted Seine.

Oft at his work, the toilsome day to cheat,
The swain still talks of those disastrous times,
When Guise's pride, and Conde's ill-starr'd heat,
Taught Christian seal to authorize their crimes:

Oft to his children sportive on the grass
Does dreadful tales of worn Tradition tell;
Oft points to Epernay's ill-fated pass,
Where force thrice triumph'd, and where Biron fell.

O dire effetts of war!—may evermore

Through this sweet vale the voice of discord cease !
A British bard to Gallia's fertile shore
Can wish the blessings of eternal peace.

Yet say, ye monks (beneath whose moss-grown seat,
Within whose cloister'd cells th' indebted Muse
Awhile sojourns, for meditation meet,
And these loose thoughts in pensive strain pursues,)

Avails it aught, that War's rude tumults spare '
Yon cluster'd vineyard, or yon golden field,
If, niggards to yourselves, and fond of care,
You slight the joys their copious treasures yield ?

Avails it aught, that Nature's liberal hand
With every blessing grateful man can know,
Clothes the rich bosom of yon smiling land,
The mountain's sloping side, or pendant brow

If meager Famine paint your pallid cheek,
If breaks the midnight bell your hours of rest,
If, 'midst heart-chilling damps, and winter bleak,
You shun the cheerful bowl, and moderate feast ?

Look forth, and be convinc'd! 'tis Nature pleads,
Her ample volume opens on your view, . -
The simple-minded swain, who running reads,
Feels the glad truth, and is it hid from you ?

Look forth, and be convinc'd! Yon prospects wide
To Reason's ear, how forcibly they speak,
Compar'd with those how dull is letter'd Pride,
And Austin's babbling Eloquence how weak!

Temp'rance, not Abstinence, in every bliss
Is Man's true joy, and therefore Heaven's command:
The wretch who riots thanks his God amiss:
Who starves, rejects the bounties of his hand.

Mark, while the Marnc in yon full channel glides,
How smooth his course, how Nature smiles around !
But should impetuous torrents swell his tides,
The fairy landskip sinks in oceans drown'd.

Nor less disastrous, should his thrifty urn
Neglected leave the once well-water'd land,
To dreary wastes yon paradise would turn,
Polluted ooze, or heaps of barren sand.

ELEGY II.

ON THE
MAUSOLEUM OF AUGUSTUS.

TO THE RIGHT HONORABLE

GEORGE BUSSY VILLIERS, VISC. VILLIERS,
[Now Earl of Jertey.]

WRITTEN AT ROME, 1756.

By the Same,

AMID these mould'ring walls, this marble round,
Where slept the Heroes of the Julian name,
Say, shall we linger still in thought profound,

And meditate the mournful paths to fame?

What though no cypress shades, in funeral rows,
No sculptur'd urns, the last records of Fate,
O'er the shrunk terrace wave their baleful boughs,
Or breathe in storied emblems of the great;

Yet not with heedless eye will we survey
The scene though chang'd, nor negligently tread;
These variegated walks, however gay,
Were once the silent mansions of the dead.

In every shrub, in every flow'ret's bloom
That paints with different hues yon smiling plain,
Some Hero's ashes issue from the tomb
And live a vegetative life again.

For matter dies not as the Sages say,
But shifts to other forms the pliant mass,
When the free spirit quits its cumb'rous clay,
And sees, beneath, the rolling Planets pass.

Perhaps, my Villiers, for I sing to Thee,
Perhaps, unknowing of the bloom it gives,
In yon fair scion of Apollo's tree
The sacred dust of young Marcellus lives.

Pluck not the leaf—'twere sacrilege to wound.
Th' ideal memory of so sweet a shade;
In these sad seats an early grave he found,
And the first rites to gloomy Dis convey'd.

Witness thou Field of Mars, that oft hadst known

His youthful triumphs in the mimic war,
Thou heard'st the heart-felt universal groan
When o'er thy bosom roll'd the funeral car.

Witness thou Tuscan stream, where oft he glow'd
In sportive strugglings with th' opposing wave,
Fast by the recent tomb thy waters flow'd
While wept the wise, the virtuous, and the brave.

O lost too soon!—yet why lament a fate
By thousands envied, and by Heaven approv'd?
Rare is the boon to those of longer date
To live, to die, admir'd, esteem'd, belov'd,

Weak are our judgments, and our passions warm,
And slowly dawns the radiant morn of truth,
Our expectations hastily we form,
And much we pardon to ingenuous youth.

Too oft we satiate on th' applause we pay
To rising Merit, and resume the Crown;
Full many a blooming genius, snatch'd away,
Has fall'n lamented who had liv'd unknown.

For hard the task, O Villiers, to sustain
The important burthen of an early fame;
Each added day some added worth to gain,
Prevent each wish, and answer every claim.

Be thou Marcellus, with a length of days I
But O remember, whatsoe'er thou art,
The most exalted breath of human praise
To please indeed must echo from the heart.

Though thou be brave, be virtuous, and be wise,
By all, like him, admir'd, esteem'd, belov'd,
'Tis from within alone true Fame can rise,
The only happy is the Self-approv'd.

ELEGY III.

TO THE RIGHT HON,

GEO. SIMON HARCOURT, VISC. NEWNHAM,
[Now Karl Harcourt.]

WRITTEN AT KOMI, 1756.

By the Same,

YES, noble Youth, 'tis true; the softer arts,
The sweetly-sounding string, and pencil's power,
Have warm'd to rapture even heroic hearts,
And taught the rude to wonder, and adore.

For beauty charms us, whether she appears.
In blended colors; or to soothing sound
Attunes her voice; or fair proportion wears
In yonder swelling dome's harmonious round.

All, all she charms; but not alike to all
Tis given to revel in her blissful bower;
Coercive ties, and Reason's powerful call,
Bid some but taste the sweets, which some devour.

When Nature govern'd, and when Man was young,

Perhaps at will th untutor'd Savage rov'd,
Where waters murmur'd, and where clusters hung
He fed, and slept beneath the shade he lov'd.

But since the Sage's more sagacious mind,
By Heaven's permission, or by Heaven's command,
To polish states his social laws assign'd,
And general good on partial duties plann'd;

Nor for ourselves our vagrant steps we bend
As heedless Chance, or wanton Choice ordain;
On various stations various tasks attend,
And men are *born* to trifle or to reign.

As chaunts the woodman whilst the Dryads weep,
And falling forests fear th' uplifted blow,
As chaunts the shepherd, while he tends his sheep,
Or weaves to pliant forms the osier bough;

To me 'tis given, whom Fortune loves to lead
Through humbler toils to life's sequester'd bowers,
To me 'tis given to wake th' amusive reed,
And sooth with song the solitary hours.

But Thee superior soberer toils demand,
Severer paths are thine of patriot fame;
Thy birth thy friends, thy king, thy native land,
Have given thee honors, and have each their claim.

Then nerve with fortitude thy feeling breast –
Each wish to combat, and each pain to bear;
Spurn with disdain th' inglorious love of rest,
Nor let the syren Ease approach thine ear.

Beneath yon cypress shade's eternal green,
See prostrate Rome her wond'rous story tell,
Mark how she rose the world's imperial queen,
And tremble at the prospect how she fell 1

Not that my rigid precepts would require
A painful struggling with each adverse gale,
Forbid thee listen to th' enchanting Lyre,
Or turn thy steps from Fancy's flowery vale.

Whate'er of Greece in sculptur'd brass survives,
Whate'er of Rome in mould'ring arcs remains
Whate'er of Genius on the canvass lives,
Or flows in polish'd verse, or airy strains,

Be these thy leisure; to the chosen few, .
Who dare excel, thy fost'ring aid afford;
Their arts, their magic powers with honors due
Exalt; but be thyself what they record.

ELEGY IV.

TO AN

OFFICER,

WRITTEN AT ROME, 1756.

By the Same.

FROM Latian fields, the mansions of Renown,
Where fix'd the Warrior God his fated seat;

Where infant Heroes learnt the martial frown,
And little hearts for genuine glory beat;

What for any friend, my soldier, shall I frame?
What nobly-glowing verse that breathes of arms,
To point his radiant path to deathless fame,
By great examples, and terrific charms?

Qiiirinus first, with bold, collected bands,
The sinewy sons of strength, for empire strove
Beneath his thunder bow'd th' astonish'd lands,
And temples rose to Mars, and to Feretrian Jove.

War taught contempt of death, contempt of pain,
And hence the Fabii, hence the Decii come:
War urg'd the slaughter, though she wept the slain,
Stern War, the rugged nurse of virtuous Rome

But not from antique fables will I draw,
To fire thy feeling soul, a dubious aid,
Though now, ev'n now, they strike with rev'rent awe,
By Poets or Historians sacred made..

Nor yet to thee the babbling Muse shall tell
What mighty kings with all their legions wrought,
What cities sunk, and storied nations fell
When Caesar, Titus, or when Trajan fought.

From private worth, and Fortune's private ways
Whilst o'er yon hill, th' exalted Trophy shows
To what vast heights of incorrupted praise
The great, the self-ennobled Marius rose.

From steep Arpinum's rock-invested shade,
From hardy Virtue's emulative school,
His daring flight th' expanding
Genius made, And by obeying nobly learnt to rule.

Abash'd, confounded, stern Iberia groan'd,
And Afric trembled to her utmost coasts;
When the proud land its destin'd Conqueror own'd
In the new Consul, and his veteran hosts.

Yet chiefs are madmen, and Ambition weak,
And mean the joys the laurePd harvests yield,
If Virtue fail. Let Fame, let Envy speak
Of Capsa's walls, and Sextia's wat'ry field.

But sink for ever, in oblivion cast,
Dishonest triumphs, and ignoble spoils.
Minturnae's Marsh severely paid at last
The guilty glories gain'd in civil broils.

Nor yet his vain contempt the Muse shall praise
For scenes of polish'd life, and letter'd worth;
The steel-ribb'd Warrior wants not Envy's ways
To darken theirs, or call his merits forth.

Witness yon Cimbrian Trophies!—Marius, there
Thy ample pinion found a space to fly;
As the plum'd eagle soaring sails in air,
In upper air, and scorns a middle sky.

Thence too thy country claim'd thee for her own,
And bade the Sculptor's toil thy acts adorn,
To teach in characters of living stone

Eternal lessons to the youth unborn.

For wisely Rome her warlike Sons rewards
With the sweet labors of her Artist's hands;
He wakes her Graces, who her empire guards,
And both Minervas join in willing bands.

O why, Britannia, why untrophied pass
The patriot deeds thy godlike Sons display,
Why breathes on high no monumental brass,
Why swells no Arc to grace Culloden's Day

Wait we 'till faithless France submissive bow
Beneath that Hero's delegated spear,
Whose lightning smote Rebellion's haughty brow,
And scatter'd her vile rout with horror in the rear?

O Land of Freedom, Land of Arts, assume
That graceful dignity thy merits claim;
Exalt thy heroes like imperial Rome,
And build their virtues on their love of fame.

So shall the modest worth, which checks my friend,
Forget its blush when rous'd by Glory's charms;
From breast to breast the generous warmth descend,
And still new trophies rise, at once, to Arts and Arms.

ELEGY V,

TO

A FRIEND SICK.

WRITTEN AT ROME, 1756..

By the Same.

'TWAS in this isle, O Wright, indulge my lay,
Whose naval form divides the Tuscan flood,
In the bright dawn of her illustrious day
Rome fix'd her temple to the healing God,

Here stood his altars, here his arm he bar'd,
And round his mystic staff the serpent twin'd,
Through crowded portals hymns of praise were heard,
And victims bled, and sacred seers divin'd.

On every breathing wall, on every round
Of column, swelling with proportion'd grace
Its stated seat some votive tablet found,
And storied wonders dignified the place.

Oft from the balmy blessings of repose,
And the cool stillness of the night's deep shade,
To light and health th' exulting Votarist rose,
Whilst fancy work'd with med'cine's powerful aid.

Oft in his dreams (no longer clogg'd with fears

Of some broad torrent, or some headlong steep,
With' each dire form Imagination wears
When harrass'd Nature sinks in turbid sleep)

Oft in his dreams he saw diffusive day
Through bursting glooms its cheerful beams extend;
On billowy clouds saw sportive Genii play,
And bright Hygeia from her heaven descend.

What marvel then, that man's o'erflowing mind
Should wreath-bound columns raise, and altars fair,
And grateful offerings pay, to Powers so kind,
Though fancy-form'd, and creatures of the Air.

Who that has writh'd beneath the scourge of pain,
Or felt the burthen'd languor of disease,
But would with joy the slightest respite gain;
And idolize the hand which lent him ease

To thee, my friend, unwillingly to thee,
For truths like these the anxious Muse appeals.
Can Memory answer from affliction free,,
Or speaks the sufferer what, I fear, he feels?

No, let me hope ere this in Romely grove
Hygeia revels with the blooming Spring,
Ere this the vocal seats the Muses love
With hymns of praise, like Paeon's temple, ring.

It was not written in the book of Fate
That, wand'ring far from Albion's sea-girt plain,
Thy distant Friend should mourn thy shorter date,
And tell to alien woods and streams his pain.

It was not written. Many a year shall roll,
If aught th' inspiring Muse aright presage,
Of blameless intercourse from Soul to Soul,
And friendship well matur'd from Youth to Age

ELEGY VI.

TO

ANOTHER FRIEND.

WRITTEN AT ROME, 1756.

By the same.

BEHOLD, my Friend, to this small orb confined
The genuine features of Aurelius' face;
The father, friend, and lover of his kind,
Shrunk to a narrow coin's contracted space.

Not so his fame; for erst did heaven ordain
Whilst seas should waft us, and whilst suns should warm,
On tongues of men, the friend of man should reign,
And in the arts he lov'd the patron charm.

Oft as amidst the mould'ring spoils of Age,
His moss-grown monuments my steps pursue
Oft as my eye revolves the historic page,
Where pass his generous acts in fair review.

Imagination grasps at many things,
Which men, which angels might with rapture see;

Then turns to humbler scenes its safer wings,
And, blush not whilst I speak it, thinks on thee.

With all that firm benevolence of mind,
Which pities, whilst it blames, th' unfeeling vain,
With all that active zeal to serve mankind,
That tender suffering for another's pain,

Why wert not thou to thrones imperial rais'd?
Did heedless Fortune slumber at thy birth,
Or on thy virtues with indulgence gaz'd,
And gave her grandeur to her sons of earth?

Happy for thee, whose less distinguish'd sphere
Now cheers in private the deiigfeled eye
For -calm Confent, and smiling Ease are there,
And, Heav'n's divinest gift, sweet .Liberty,

Happy for me on life's serener flood
Who sail, by talents as by choice restrain
Else had I only shar'd the general good,
And lost the friend the universe had gain'd,

ELEGY VII.

TO A
YOUNG NOBLEMAN
[LORD JOHN CAVENDISH.]
Leaving the University.

BY THE REV. WILLIAM MASON, M.A.

ERE yet, ingenuous Youth, thy steps retire From

Cam's smooth margin, and the peaceful vale,
Where Science call'd thee to her studious quire,
And met thee musing in her cloysters pale;

Oh! let thy friend (and may he boast the name)
Breathe from his artless reed one parting lay;
A lay like this thy early Virtues claim,
And this let voluntary Friendship pay.

Yet know, the time arrives, the dangerous time,
When all those Virtues, opening now so fair
Transplanted to the world's tempestuous clime,
Must learn each Passion's boist'rous breath to bear.

There, if Ambition pestilent and pale,
Or Luxury should taint their vernal glow;
If cold Self-interest, with her chilling gale,
Should blast th' unfolding blossoms ere they blow;

If mimic hues, by Art, or Fashion spread,
Their genuine, simple coloring should supply,
Ohl with them may these laureate honors fade;
And with them (if it can) my Friendship die.

Then do not blame, if, tho thyself inspire,
Cautious I strike the panegyric string;
The Muse full oft pursues a meteor fire,
And, vainly vent'rous, soars on waxen wing.

Too actively awake at Friendship's voice,
The Poet's bosom pours the fervent strain,
Till sad Reflection blames the hasty choice,
And oft invokes Oblivion's aid in vain.

Call we the Shade of POPE, from that blest bower
Where thron'd he sits with many a tuneful Sage;
Ask, if he ne'er bemoans that hapless hour
When ST. JOHN'S name illumin'd Glory's page?

Ask, if the wretch, who dar'd his mem'ry stain,
Ask, if his country's, his religion's foe
Deserv'd the meed that MARLBRO' fail'd to gain,
The deathless meed, he only could bestow?

The Bard will tell thee, the misguided praise
Clouds the celestial sunshine of his breast;
Ev'n now, repentant of his erring Lays,
He heaves a sigh amid the realms of rest.

If POPE thro' Friendship fill'd, indignant view,
Yet pity DRy Den \ hark, Whene'er he sings,
How Adulation drops her Courtly dew
On titled Rhymers, and inglorious Kings

See, from the depths of his exhaustless mine,
His glittering stores the tuneful Spendthrift throws
Where Fear, or Interest bids, behold they shine;
Now grace a CROMWELL'S, now a CHARLES'S brows.

Born with too generous, or too mean a heart,
DRYDEN! in vain to thee those stores were lent:
Thy sweetest numbers but a trifling Art;
Thy strongest di&ion idly eloquent.

The simplest Lyre, if Truth direct its
Lays, Warbles a melody ne'er heard from thine:

Not to disgust with false, or venal praise,
Was PARNELL'S modest fame, and may be mine.

Go then, my Friend, nor let thy candid breast
Condemn me, if I check the plausive string;
Go to the wayward world; compleat the rest ;
Be, what the purest Muse would wish to sing.

Be still thyself ; that open path of Truth,
Which led thee here, let Manhood firm pursue \
Retain the sweet simplicity of Youth,
And, all thy virtue dictates, dare to do.

Still scorn, with conscious pride, the mask of
Art On vice's front let fearful caution lower,
And teach the diffident, discreeter part
Of knaves that plot, and fools that fawn for Power.

So, round thy brow when Age's honors spread,
When Death's cold tund unstrings thy MASON' lyre,

When the green turf lies lightly on his head,
Thy worth shall some superior bard inspire:

He, to the amplest bounds of Time's domain,
On Rapture's plume shall give thy Name to fly;
For trust, with reverence trust this Sabine strain
" The Muse forbids the virtuous Man to die."

ELEGY VIll.

WRITTEN IN THE

GARDEN OF A FRIEND.
[THE REV. MR. WOOD OF INDSOR.]

By the Same,

WHILE o'er my head this laurel-woven bower
Its arch of glittering verdure wildly flings,
Can Fancy slumber ? can the tuneful Power,
That rules my lyre, neglect her wonted strings ?

No; if the blighting East deform'd the plain,
If this gay bank no balmy sweets exhal'd,
Still should the grove re-echo to my strain,
And friendship prompt the theme, where beauty fail'd.

For he, whose careless art this foliage drest,
Who bad these twisting braids of woodbine bend,
He first, with truth and virtue, taught my breast
Where best to chuse, and best to fix a friend.

How well does Mem'ry note the golden day,
What time, reclin'd in Marg'ret's studious glade,
My mimic reed first tun'd the Dorian Lay,
" Unseen, unheard, beneath an hawthorn shade"

'Twas there we met; the Muses hail'm the hour;
The same desires, the same ingenuous arts
Inspir'd us both ; we own'd, and blest the power

That join'd at once our studies, and our hearts.

Oh 1 since those days, when Science spread the feast,
When emulative Youth its relish lent,
Say, has one genuine Joy e'er warm'd my breast
Enough; if Joy was his, be mine Content.

To thirst for praise his temperate Youth forbore
He fondly wish'd not for a Poet's name;
Much did he love the Muse, but Quiet more,
And, tho' he might command, he slighted Fame.

Hither, in manhood's prime, he wisely fled
From all that Folly, all that Pride approves;
To this soft scene a tender Partner led;
This laurel shade was witness to their loves.

" Begone," he cry'd, " Ambition's air-drawn plan;
Hence with perplexing pomp, unwieldy wealth:
Let me not seem, but be the happy man,
Possest of Love, of Competence, and Health."

Smiling he spake, nor did the Fates withstand;
In rural arts the peaceful moments flew:
Say, lovely Lawn ! that felt his forming hand
How soon thy surface shone with vender new.;

How soon obedient FLORA brought her store,
And o'er thy breast a shower of fragrance flung:
VERTUMNUS came; his earliest blooms he bore,
And thy rich sides with waving purple hung:

Then to the sight, he call'd yon stately spire,

He pierc'd th* opposing oak's luxuriant shade;
Bad yonder crowding hawthorns low retire,
Nor veil the glories of the golden mead.

Hail, sylvan wonders, hail and hail the hand,
Whose native taste thy native charms display'd
And taught one little acre to command
Each envied happiness of scene, and shade.

Is there a hill, whose distant azure bounds
The ample range of Scarsdale's proud domain,
A mountain hoar, that yon wild Peak surrounds
But lends a willing beauty to thy plain?

And, lo! in yonder path I spy my friend;
He looks the guardian genius of the grove,
Mild as the fabled Form that whilom deign'd,
At MILTON'S call, in Harefield'6 haunts to rove.

Blest Spirit, come! tho pent in mortal mould,
I'll yet invoke thee by that purer name;
Oh come, a portion of thy bliss unfold,
Erom Folly's maze my wayward step reclaim.

Too long, alas, my inexperienc'd youth,
Misled by flattering Fortune's specious tale,
Has left the rural reign of Peace, and Truth,
The huddling brook, cool cave, and whispering vale.

Won to the world, a candidate for praise,
Yet, let me boast, by no ignoble art,
Too oft the public ear has heard my lays,
Too much its vain applause has touch'd my heart;

But now, ere Custom binds his powerful chains,
Come, from the base enchanter set me free,
While yet my soul its first, best taste retains,
Recall that soul to reason, peace, and thee.

Teach me, like thee, to muse on Nature's page,
To mark each wonder in Creation's plan,
Each mode of being trace, and, humbly sage,
Deduce from these the genuine powers of Man

Of Man, while warm'd with reason's purer ray,
No tool of policy, no dupe to pride;
Before vain Science led his taste astray ;
When conscience was his law, and God his guide.

This let me learn, and learning let me live
The lesson o'er. From that great Guide of Truth
Oh may my suppliant soul the boon receive
To tread thro' age the footsteps of thy youth.

ELEGY IX.

TO
THE REV. MR. HURD,
[NOW BISHOP OF WORCETER.]

By the Same.

FRIEND of my youth, who, when the willing Muse
Stream'd o'er my breast her warm poetic rays,
Saw'st the fresh seeds their vital powers diffuse,
And fed'st them with the fost'ring dew of praise!

Whate'er the produce of th' unthrifty soil,
The leaves, the flowers, the fruits, to thee belong:
The labourer earns the wages of his toil;
Who form'd the Poet, well may claim the song.

Yes, 'tis my pride to own, that taught by thee
My conscious soul superior flights essay'd;
Learnt from thy lore the Poets dignity,
And spurn'd the hirelings of the rhyming trade.

Say, scenes of Science, say, thou haunted stream!
(For oft my Muse-led steps did'st thou behold)
How on thy banks I rifled every theme,
That Fancy fabled in her age of gold.

How oft' I cry'd, " Oh come, thou tragic Queen!
March from thy Greece with firm majestic tread !
Such as when Athens saw thee fill her scene,
When Sophocles thy choral Graces led:
"Saw thy proud pall its purple length devolve ;
Saw thee uplift the glitt'ring dagger high;
Ponder with fixed brow thy deep resolve,
Prepar'd to strike, to triumph, and to die.

" Bring then to Britain's plain that choral throng
Display thy buskin'd pomp, thy golden lyre:
Give her historic Forms the soul of song,
And mingle Attic art with SHAKSPERE'S fire."

" Ab, what, food boy, dost thou presume to claim ?"
The Muse reply'd: " Mistaken suppliant, know
To light in SHAKSPERE'S breast the dazzling flame

Exhausted all PARMASSUS could bestow.

True Ait remains; and,' if from has bright page
Thy mimic power one vivid beam cas seize,

Proceed ; and to that best of tasks engage,
Which lends at once to profit and to please,"

She spake; and Harewood's Towers spontaneous rose;
Soft virgin warblings echo'd thro' the grove;
And fair ELFRIDA pour'd forth all her woes,
The hapless pattern of connubial Love.

More awful scenes old Mona next display'd;
Her caverns gloom'd, her forests wav'd on high,
While flam'd within their consecrated shade
The Genius stern of British liberty.

And see, my HURD ! to thee those scenes consign'd;
Oh 1 take and stamp them with thy honor'd name,
Around the page be friendship's chaplet twin'd ;
And, if they find the road to honest Fame,

Perchance the candor of some nobler age
May praise the Bard, who bad gay Folly bear
Her cheap applauses to the busy stage,
And leave him pensive Virtue's silent tear:

Chose too to consecrate his fav'rite strain
To Him, who grac'd by ev'ry liberal art,
That best might shine among the learned train,
Yet more excell'd in morals and in heart:

Whose equal mind could see vain fortune shower
Her flimsy favors on the fawning crew,
While, in low Thurcaston's sequester'd bower,
She fixt him distant from Promotion's view:

Yet, shelter'd there by calm Contentment's wing,
Pleas'd he could smile, and, with sage HOOKER'S eye,
" See from his mother earth God's blessings spring,
And eat his bread in peace and privacy."

ELEGY X.

THE

VISIONS OF FANCY,

IN FOUR ELEGIES. WRITTEN IN MDCCLXII.

BY THE REV. JOHN LANGHORNE, D.D.

La Raison scait que c'est un Songe,
Mais elle en saisit les douceurs:
Elle a besoin de ces fantomes,
Presque cous les Flaisirs des Hommes
Ne sont que de douces Erreurs. Gresest.

CHILDREN of FANCY, whither are ye fled ?
Where have ye borne those Hope-enliven'd
Hours, That once with myrtle garlands bound my head,
That once bestrew'd my vernal path with flowers ?

In yon fair vale, where blooms the beechen grove,
Where winds the slow wave thro' the flowery plain,

To these fond arms you led the Tyrant LOVE,
With FEAR and HOPE and FOLLY in his train.

My lyre, that, left at careless distance, hung
Light on some pale branch of the osier shade,
To lays of amorous blandishment you strung,
And o'er my sleep the lulling music play'd.

" Rest, gentle youth! while on the quivering breeze
Slides to thine ear this softly breathing strain;
Sounds that move smoother than the steps of ease,
And pour oblivion in the ear of pain.

" In this fair vale eternal spring shall Smile,
And TIME unenvious crown each roseate hour;
Eternal joy shall every care beguile,
Breathe in each gale, and bloom in every flower.

" This silver stream, that down its crystal way
Frequent has led thy musing steps along,
Shall, still the same, in sunny mazes play,
And with its murmurs melodise thy song.

" Unfading green shall these fair groves adorn
Those living meads immortal flowers unfold;
In rosy smiles shall rise each blushing morn,
And every evening close in clouds of gold.

" The tender LOVES that watch thy slumbering rest,
And round thee flowers and balmy myrtles strew,
Shall charm, thro all approaching life, thy breast,
With joys for ever pure, for ever new.

" The genial power that speeds the golden dart,
Each charm of tender passion shall inspire;
With fond affection fill the mutual
heart, And feed the flame of over-young desire.

Come gentle LOVES ! your myrtle garlands bring ;
The smiling bower with cluster'd roses spread;
Come gentle AIRS I with incense-dropping wing
The breathing sweets of vernal odor shed.

" Hark, as the strains of swelling music rise,
How the notes vibrate on the fav'ring gale !
Auspicious glories beam along the skies,
And powers unseen the happy moments hail !

" Extatic hours! so every distant day
Like this serene on downy wings shall move;
Rise crown'd with joys that triumph o'er decay,
The faithful joys of FANCY and of LOVE."

ELEGY THE SECOND,

AND were they vain, those soothing lays ye sung ?
Children of FANCY ! yes, your song was vain;
On each soft air though rapt ATTENTION hung,
And SILENCE listen'd on the sleeping plain.

The strains yet vibrate on my ravisht ear,
And still to smile the mimic beauties seem,
Though now the visionary scenes appear
Like the faint traces of a vanishr dream.

Mirror of life! the glories thus depart

Of all that YOUTH and LOVE and FANCY frame,
When painful ANGUISH speeds the piercing dart,
Or ENVY blasts the blooming flowers of FAME.

Nurse of wild wishes, and of fond desires,
The prophetess of FORTUNE, false and vain,
To scenes where PEACE in RUIN'S arms expires
Fallacious HOPE deludes her hapless train.

Go, Syren, go thy charms on others try;
My beaten bark at length has reach'd the shore:
Yet on the rock my dropping garments lie;
And let me perish, if I trust thee more.

Come gentle QUIET ! long-neglected maid!
O come, and lead me to thy mossy cell;
There unregarded in the peaceful shade,
With calm REPOSE and SILENCE let me dwell

Come happier hours of sweet unanxious rest,
When all the struggling passions shall subside;
When PEACE shall clasp me to her plumy breast,
And smoothe my silent minutes as they glide.

But chief, thou goddess of the thoughtless eye,
Whom never cares or passions discompose,
O blest INSENSIBILITY be nigh,
And with thy soothing hand my weary eyelids close.

Then shall the cares of love and glory cease,
And all the fond anxieties of fame;
Alike regardless in the arms of PEACE,
If these extol, or those debase a name.

In LYTTELTON though all the muses praise,
His generous praise shall then delight no more,
Nor the sweet magic of his tender lays
Shall touch the bosom which it charm'd before.

Nor then, tho' MALICE, with insidious guise
Of friendship, ope the unsuspecting breast;
Nor then, tho' ENVY broach her blackening lies,
Shall these deprive me of a moment's rest.

O state to be desir'd! when hostile rage
Prevails in human more than savage haunts;
When man with man eternal war will wage,
And never yield that mercy which he wants.

When dark DESIGN invades the chearful hour,
And draws the heart with social freedom warm
Its cares, its wishes, and its thoughts to pour,
Smiling insidious with the hopes of harm.

Vain man, to other's failings still severe,
Yet not one foible in himself can find;
Another's faults to FOLLY'S eye are clear,
But to her own e'en WISDOM'S self is blind.

O let me still, from these low follies free,
This sordid malice, and inglorious strife,
Myself the subject of my censure be,
And teach my heart to comment on my life,

With thee, PHILOSOPHY, still let me dwell,
My tutor'd mind from vulgar meanness save;

Bring PEACE, bring QUIET to my humble cell,
And bid them lay the green turf on my grave.

BRIGHT o'er the green hills rose the morning ray,
The wood-lark's song resounded on the plain ;
Fair NATURE felt the warm embrace of day,
And smtl'd thro'- all her animated reign.

When young DELIGHT, of HOPE and FANCY born
His head on tufted wild thyme half-reclin'd,
Caught the gay colors of the orient morn,
And thence of life this picture vain design'd.

" O born to thoughts, to pleasures more sublime
Than beings of inferior nature prove I
To triumph in the golden hours of TIME,
And feel the charms of fancy and of love !

" High-favor'd man I for him unfolding fair
In orient light this native landscape smiles ;
For him sweet HOPE disarms the hand of care,
Exalts his pleasures, and his grief beguiles.

" Blows not a blossom on the breast of SPRING,
Breathes not a gale along the bending mead,
Trills not a songster of the soaring wing,
But fragrance, health and melody succeed.

" O let me still with simple NATURE live,
My lowly field-flowers on her altar lay,
Enjoy the blessings that she meant to give,
And calmly waste my inoffensive day I

" No titled name, no envy-teasing dome,
No glittering wealth my tutor'd wishes crave ;
So HEALTH and PEACE be near my humble home,
A cool stream murmur, and a green tree wave.

" So may the sweet EUTERPE not disdain
At Eve's chaste hour her silver lyre to brings;
The Muse of pity wake her soothing strain,
And tune to sympathy the trembling string.

" Thus glide the pensive moments, o'er the vale
While floating shades of dusky night descend :
Not left untold the lover's tender tale, —
Nor unenjoy'd the heart-enlarging friend.

" To love and friendship flow the social bowl
To attic wit and elegance of mind ;
To all the native beauties of the soul,
The simple charms of truth, and sense refin'd

" Then to explore whatever ancient sage
Studious from nature's early volume drew,
To chase sweet FICTION thro' her golden age,
And mark how fair the sun-flower, Science, blew

" Haply to catch some spark of eastern fire,
Hesperian fancy, or *Aonian* ease ;
Some melting note from SAPPHO'S tender lyre,
Some strain that LOVE and PHOEBUS taught to please.

" When waves the grey light o'er the mountain's head,
Then let me meet the morn's first beauteous ray ;
Carelessly wander from my sylvan shed,

And catch the sweet breath of the rising day.

" Nor seldom, loitering as I muse along,
Mark from what flower the breeze its sweetness bore}
Or listen to the labour-soothing song
Of bees that range the thymy uplands o'er.

" Slow let me climb the mountain's airy brow,
The green height gain'd, in museful rapture lie,
Sleep to the murmur of the woods below,
Or look on NATURE with a lover's eye.

" Delightful hours! O, thus for ever flow;
Led by fair FANCY round the varied year:
So shall my breast with native raptures glow,
Nor feel one pang from folly, pride, or fear.

" Firm be my heart to NATURE and to TRUTH,
Nor vainly wander from their dictates sage;
So JOY shall triumph on the brows of youth,
So HOPE shall smooth the dreary paths of age."

ELEGY THE FOURTH.

OH ! yet, ye dear, deluding visions stay!
Fond hopes, of INNOCENCE and FANCY born!
For you I'll cast these waking thoughts away,
For one wild dream of life's romantic morn.

Ah! no: the sunshine o'er each object spread
By flattering HOPE, the flowers that blew so fair,
Like the gay gardens of ARM ID A fled,
And vanish'd from the powerful rod of CARE.

So the poor pilgrim, who in rapturous thought
Plans his dear journey to **Lorettd's** shrine,
Seems on his way by guardian seraphs brought,
Sees aiding angels favour his design.

Ambrosial blossoms, such of old as blew
By those fresh founts on Eden's happy plain,
And **Sharon's** roses all his passage strew:
So FANCY dreams; but FANCY'S dreams are vain.

Wasted and weary on the mountain's side,
His way unknown, the hapless pilgrim lies,
Or take some ruthless robber for his guide,
And prone beneath his cruel sabre dies,

Life's morning-landscape gilt with orient light,
Where HOPE and JOY and FANCY hold their reign,
The grove's green wave, the blue stream sparkling bright,
The blithe hours dancing round **Hyperion's** wain,

In radiant colours YOUTH'S free hand pourtrays,
Then holds the flattering tablet to his eye;
Nor thinks how soon the vernal grove decays,
Nor sees the dark cloud gathering o'er the sky

Hence FANCY conquer'd by the dart of PAIN,
And wandering far from her Platonic shade,
Mourns o'er the ruins of her transient reign,
Nor unrepining sees her visions fade.

Their parent banish'd, hence her children fly,
The fairy race that fill'd her festive train;

JOY tears his wreath, and HOPE inverts her eye,
And FOLLY wonders that her dream was vain.

ELEGY XI.

LIBERTY:

Inscribed to

MISS LOGGIN.

BY MRS. DARWALL,

[Late Miss Whately.]

FEIGNED TO BE WRITTEN FROM THE HAPPY VALLEY OF AMBARA.

To you, Eliza, be these lays consign'd,
Who blest in Freedom's fair dominions live:
While I, alas! am pompously confin'd,
Bereft of every joy the world can give,

In vain for me the blushing flow'rets bloom,c
A spring eternal decks the fragrant shade;
In vain the dewy myrtle breathes perfume,
And sounds angelic echo through the glade.

The marble palaces, and glittering spires,
What are they? Pageant glare, and empty show:
Ah 1 how unequal to my fond desires!
Which tell me—Freedom makes a heaven below.

Pensive I range these ever-verdant groves,

And sigh responsive to the murmuring stream;
While woodland warblers chant their happy loves,
Dear Liberty is wretched Myra's theme.

The velvet lawns diversify'd with flowers
In sweet succession every morn the same:
Fresh gales that breathe through amaranthine bowers,
And every charm inventive Art can frame.

Here fondly vie to crown this favoured place:
And here, to smooth captivity a prey,
Each royal child of Abyssinian race
Consumes the vacant inauspicious day.

Though festive mirth awake the laughing morn
And guiltless revels lead the dancing hours;
Though purling rills the fertile meads adorn,
And the wild rock its spicy product pours:

Yet what are these to fill a boundless mind?
Though gay each scene appear, tis still the same;
Variety—in vain I hope to find;
Variety, thou dear, but distant name!

With pleasure cloy'd, and sick of tasteless ease,
No sweet alternatives my spirits chear;
Joys oft repeated lose their power to please,
And harmony grows discord to my ear.

Blest Freedom! how I long with thee to rove,
Where varying Nature all her charms displays;
To range the sun-burnt hill, the rifted grove,
And trace the silver current's winding maze

Free as the wing'd inhabitants of air,
Who distant climes and various seasons see,
Regions—though not, like soft Ambara, fair;
"Yet blest with change, and crown'd with Liberty.

Vain wish 1 these rocks, whose summits pierce the skies,
With frowning aspect tell me—Hope is vain:
Till, freed by death, the purer spirit flies,
Here wretched Myra's destin'd to remain

ELEGY XII.

TO —

BY MISS CARTER.

How sweet the calm of this sequester'd shore,
Where ebbing waters musically roll:
And Solitude and silent Eve restore
The philosophic temper of the soul.

The sighing gale, whose murmurs lull to rest
The busy tumult of declining day,
To sympathetic quiet soothes the breast,
And every wild emotion dies away.

Farewell the objects of diurnal care,
Your task be ended with the setting sun :
Let all be undisturb'd vacation here,
While o'er yon wave ascends the peaceful Moon.

What beauteous visions o'er the soften'd heart,

In this still moment all their charms diffuse,
Serener joys and brighter hopes impart,
And chear the soul with more than mortal views.

Here faithful Memory wakens all her powers,
She bids her fair ideal forms ascend,
And quick to every gladden'd thought restores
The social virtue, and the absent friend.

Come come, and with me share
The sober pleasures of this solemn scene,
While no rude tempest clouds the ruffled air,
But all, like thee, is smiling and serene.

Come, while the cool, the solitary hours
Each foolish care, and giddy wish control,
With all thy foft persuasion's wonted powers,
Beyond the stars transport my listening soul.

Oft, when on earth detain'd by empty show,
Thy voice has taught the trifler how to rise
Taught her to look with scorn on things below,
And seek her better portion in the skies.

Come: and the sacred eloquence repeat:
The world shall vanish at its gentle sound,
Angelic forms shall visit this retreat,
And opening heaven diffuse its glories round.

ELEGY XIII.

TOMRS —.

By the Same.

WHERE are those hours, on rosy pinions borne,
Which brought to every guiltless wish success?
When Pleasure gladden'd each returning morn,
And every evening clos'd in calms of peace.

How siml'd each object, when by Friendship led,
Thro' flowery paths we wander'd unconfin'd :
Enjoy'd each airy hill, or solemn shade,
And left the bustling empty world behind.

With philosophic, social sense survey'd
The noon-day sky in brighter colors shone
And softer o'er the dewy landscape play'd
The peaceful radiance of the silent moon.

Those hours are vanished with the changing year,
And dark December clouds the summer scene :
Perhaps, alas 1 for ever vanish'd here, —
No more to bless distinguished life again.

Yet not like those by thoughtless Folly drown'd,
In blank Oblivion's sullen, stagnant deep,
Where, never more to pass their fated bound,
The ruins of neglected Being sleep.

But lasting traces mark the happier hours,
Which active zeal in life's great task employs:
Which Science from the waste of Time secures,
Or various Fancy gratefully enjoys.

O still be ours to each improvement given,
Which Friendship doubly to the heart endears:
Those hours, when banish'd hence, shall fly to heaven,
And claim the promise of eternal year's.

ELEGY XIV.

BY
THE REV. JOHN DELAP, D. D.

AH stay I—thy wand oblivious o'er my eyes
Yet wave, mild power of sleep!—my prayer is vain;
She flies, the partial nurse. of nature flies,
With all her soothing visionary train.
Then let me forth; and near yon flowering thorn
Taste heaven's pure breath; while rob'd in amber vest,
Fresh from her watery couch, the youthful morn
Steals on the slumbers of the drowsy east.

Lo, at her presence, the strong arm of toil,
With glittering sickle mows the prime of May;
While yon poor hirelings, for the mine's rude soil,
Leave to their sleeping babes their cots of clay.

With sturdy step, they cheerly whistle o'er
The path that flings across the reedy plain,
To the deep caverns of that yawning moor,
Whose shaggy breast abhors the golden grain.

There, in her green dress, nature never roves,
Spreads the gay lawn, nor lifts the lordly pine
They see |no melting clouds refresh the groves,
No living landscape drawn by hands divine.

But many a fathom from the sunny breeze,t
Their painful way in central night they wear;
Heave the pik'd axes on their bended knees,
Or, sidelong the rough quarry slowly tear.

Yet while damp vapors chill each reeking brow
How loudly laughs the jovial voice of mirth;
Pleas'd that the wages of the day allow
A social blaze to chear their evening hearth.

There the chaste housewife, with maternal care,
Her thrifty distaff plies, in grave attire;
Blest to behold her ruddy offspring wear
The full resemblance of their sturdy sire;

To spread with such coarse fare their homely board
As fits the genius of their little fate,
Free from those ills that haunt their pamper'd lord;
To be unhappy we must first be great.

In these dark caves, where heaven's paternal hand,
Far from the world their private cradle laid,
They toil secure; the storms that strike the land
With wild dismay rolijharmless o'er their head.

For who, the load of weary life to bear,
Wou'd from these murky mansions chace the slave ?

Who cease to breathe heaven's pure and chearful air,
To be but living tenants of the grave?

Yet harrass'd as they are, their face still wears
[The reverend comeliness of green old age;
No stains their mind from worldly science bears:
Their ray of knowledge gleams from nature's page.

The few plain rules her simple lessons give,
They still thro' life with pleas'd attention ply;
Their helpless offspring bid them wish to live,
Their breathless parents bid them learn to die,

And surely heaven, whose penetrating sight
Pierces the soul, and reads its inmost groan,
Must see content, with more sincere delight,
Toil in the mine, than triumph on the throne;

See Charles, more pleas'd, within the convent's gloom,
Seeking the slaves' calm nights, their temperate days,
And peaceful passage to the private tomb,
Than diadem'd with glory's crimson rays.

Ev'n the proud sage, whose deep mysterious brain
Has reason'd all the balm of hope away,
Convinc'd that learning's but ingenious pain,
Might hail their happier lot, and sighing say,

" Oh had I thus, within the dark profound,
By daily labor earn'd my daily food;
Or with yon seed man sow'd the quickening ground,
Or cleav'd with ponderous axe the groaning wood;

" Full many an hour that now, tho sped with art,
On slow and dusky pinions sullen flies,
Full many an anxious wish, or pang of heart,
That reason's boasted anodyne defies,

" Had ne'er been born. Nor had th' uneasy mind,
fent in the prison of this mortal mould,
Felt its etherial energy confin'd,
Its brightest sunshine in dark clouds enroll'd.

" But native sense her modest course had run;
Her faintly lustre untaught virtue spread;
Health crown'd my toils, and, ere the day was done,
Sound sleep beneath some alder's rustling shade.

" Then, as I stole down life's declining hill,
Here nature's gifts had furnish'd nature's needs,
The brook's cold beverage every latent ill
Had starv'd, that cloyster'd contemplation feeds.

" Till in the peaceful shade of this lone bower,
Or near yon shattered tower in silence laid,
The orient orb, that watch'd ray natal hour,
Had brightly glitter'd o'er my mouldering head."

ELEGY XV.

TO
SICKNESS.

By the Same.

How blithe the flowery graces of the Spring

From nature's wardrobe come: and hark how gay
Each glittering insect, hovering on the wing,
Sing their glad welcome} to the fields of May.

They gaze with greedy eye, each beauty o'er;
They suck the sweet breath of the blushing rose ;
Sport in the gale, or sip the rainbow shower;
Their life's short day no pause of pleasure knows.

Like their's, dread power, my cheerful morn display'd
The flattering proigise of a golden noon,
Till each gay cloud, that sportive nature spread,
Died in the gloom]of thy distempered frown.

Yes, ere I told my two and twentieth year,
Swift from thy quiver flew the deadly dart;
Harmless it pass'd 'mid many a blithe compeer,
And found its fated entrance near my heart.

Pale as I lay beneath thy ebon wand,
I saw them rove thro' pleasure's flowery field:
I saw health paint them with her rosy hand,
Eager to burst my bonds, but forc'd to yield

Yet while this mortal cot of mouldering clay
Shakes at the stroke of thy tremendous power,
Ah must the transient tenant of a day
Bear the rough blast of each tempestuous hour!

Say, shall the terrors thy pale flag unfolds,
Too rigid queen! unnerve the soul's bright powers,
Till with a joyless smile the eye beholds
Art's magic charms, and nature's fairy bowers ?

No, let me follow still those bowers among,
Her flowery footsteps., as the goddess goes
Let me just lifted 'bove th' unletter'd throng,
Read the few books the learned few compose.

And suffer, when thy awful pleasure calls
The soul to share her frail companion's smart,
Yet suffer me to taste the balm that falls
From friendship's tongue, so sweet upon the heart.

Then, tho' each trembling nerve confess thy frown,
Ev'n till this anxious being shall become
But a brief name upon a little stone,
Without one murmur I embrace my doom.

For many a virtue, shelter'd from mankind,
Lives calm with thee, and lord o'er each desire;
And many a feeble frame, whose mighty mind
Each muse has touch'd with her immortal fire.

Even he, sole terror of a venal age,
The tuneful bard, whose philosophic soul
With such bright radiance glow'd on virtue's page,
Learn'd many a lesson from thy moral school.

He too, who " mounts and keeps his distant way,"
His daring mind thy humanizing glooms.
Have temper'd with a melahcholy ray,
And taught to warble 'mid the village tombs.

Yes, goddess, to thy temple's deep recess
I come; and lay for ever at its door

The siren throng of follies numberless,
Nor wish their flatteringsongs should soothme more.

Thy decent garb shall o'er my limbs be spread,
Thy hand shall lead me to thy sober train,
Who here retir'd, with pensive pleasure tread
The silent windings of thy dark domain.

Hither the cherub Charity shall fly
From her bright orb, and brooding o'er my mind,
For misery raise a sympathizing sigh,
Pardon for foes, and love for human kind.

Then while ambition's trump, from age to age
Its slaughter'd millions boasts; while Fame shall rear
Her deathless trophies o'er the bard and sage
Be mine the widow's sigh, the orphan's prayer.

ELEGY XVI.

NIGHT.

Br MR. T.

SURROUNDED with the horrors of thy reign,
The aweful terrors of thy gloomy power,
My soul at large will now her woes complain,
And wail her miseries in this silent hour.—

Hold!—let me stop the trickling streams, which pour
Successive torrents down my flooded cheeks;
A woe like mine no common tears deplore—
'Tis Sorrow's self this briny language speaks

Speaks in the broken accent of a sigh,.
Speaks in the throbbing of a wretch's heart;
Pours her strong rhietoric through the moisten'd eye,
With thundering pathos, and a long-felt smart.

Ah!—see that shade which glides along my room
Steals by my sight in slow-stepp'd solemn pace,
Clad from the clayey wardrobe of a tomb,
In trailing robes, which cover half the place!

I think I see a well-known visage there;
I think I see—but grief forbids the rest!
Yes!—Yes! I see thee through the starting tear,
And feel thy presence on my panting breast.

Ah! dearest shade!—how oft has thy pleas'd eye
The scarce-form'd features of my frame survey'd;
When yet my only language was a cry,
Which all my hungry, thirsty wants convey'd.

When yet from, passion's swell my heart was free,
Nor knew the stimulative force of guile,—
Laughing I 'Ve play'd upon thy dancing knee,
And thy lov'd face has join'd me in a smile.

How oft has sorrow dampened all thy breast,
When thou hast heard thy fondled infant weep !
How hast thou robb'd the lengthening night of rest,
To beg descending blessings on his sleep!

Yes! thy whole soul has melted into prayer,
For streaming mercies on my infant head;

And shall my heart forget thy pious care,
Because, alas I thou 'rt mingled with the dead ;

Thou silvering moon, whose pale-complexion'd beam
Has wander'd with me through the midnight air,
And lent a cheerless, cloud bemoisten'd gleam,
To awe my anguish into dread despair ;

Ye groves, where oft my evening footsteps tread !
Lugubrious yews !—and weeding osiers round
Where black Solemnity's sad couch is spread,
And dewy horrors clothe the hallow'd ground;

Witness the plainings of my bursting heart,
Declare the echoes of my soul-torn sighs;
Those which could sadness to the Bless'd impart,
These which have pierc'd beyond the vaulted skies.

Thou kind sustainer of my wearied head!
From thee I 've sought an opiative repose,
And hop'd to still my sorrows on my bed,
Or load oblivion with a wretch's woes !

Thou dear companion of my softer hours,
When round thy neck I 've laid my nerveless arm;
When grief has weaken 'd all my manly powers,
And stripp'd thy love of every grace to charm;

How have my sorrows trickled down thy breast,
And moisten'd all the bloom upon thy cheek;
While thou hast strove to sooth my soul to rest,
And gave that balm I knew not where to seek.

Supreme Director of this world of grief!;
Unending Ruler of yon plains of light:
From thee alone descends the wish'd relief,
From thee that sun which cheers the gloom of night.

Let not compassion be forgot in heaven!
O hear the sinner! (often deaf to thee!) Hear him,
O God! and speak his faults forgiven;
Thou heart-felt penitence alone canst see I

And thou, bless'd spirit of my parent dead,
Whose care has often check'd my erring feet!
Be present with me in unbodied shade,
And still conduct me till I share thy seat!

Is my tongue silent in thy much-lov'd praise?
Does it neglect the tributary strain;
Refuse the trophied poetry to raise,
And join its horrors to the weeping train

Then let unending Sadness spread her veil,
And wrap my spirit in eternal night;
Let horrid anguish all my nerves assail,
And the grave hide me from the beaming light?

Let dreadful judgment o'er my head,
Forbidding ev'n a distant hope of rest,
If I forget to reverence thy shade,
Or blot thy memory from my sadden'd breast!

ELEGY XVII.

SPRING.

BY MR. JOHN NICHOLS.
[Inscribed to the Author of the roregoiag.]

STILL must, my friend, the briny torrent flow ?
Still must the Muse a funeral dirge rehearse ?
Still breathe thy strains in energetic woe ?
Still filial duty claim the heart-felt verse ?

No! change thy numbers ! let the Sapphic lyre
" Again invite the melting soul to peace;
With Lyric sweetness join Pindaric fire,
And emulate the prodigies of Greece !

Ah! dwell no longer on the woe-fraught page!
Cease for a while on Plato's strains to pore :
Let sprightlier themes thy studious thoughts engage,
And hail Parnassus in a lighter lore.

Blame not my counsel—'tis with kind intent—
Though dear the parent—terrible the stroke—
The mead she gain'd of years devoutly spent—
The chain, which stay'd her flight to Heavert, is broke!

'Tis friendship's force impels an unskill'd Muse,
With zeal officious, to remove thy grief;
And wilt thou still inflexibly refuse
To talk of comfort, or receive relief?

See! lovely Spring, with renovating hand,
Her blooming empire o'er the world display!
Plenty she scatters through the smiling land,
And with new raptures wakes the genial day!

See ! Nature's gifts demand thy tuneful voice !
The vernal meads thy devious steps invite ;
In Heaven-taught lays, where warbling larks rejoice,
And Philomela's trillings chear the night !

Heedful no more of Winter's dreary reign,
Of frozen slumbers, or of drifted snow,
The sportive floods their wonted channels gain,
And glide unmindful of their frigid foe !

None now are dumb !—The vegetative race
With eloquence unfathomable preac
Inanimates now wear a pleasing face;
And to mankind instructive lessons teach!

Loos'd from his rein, th' impatient courser bounds,
Neighs to the Heavens, and shares the general joy;
With savage gratitude the grove resounds ;
Love-bleating hymns the milder flocks employ

Nor is man silent!—Chearful as the day,
Salubrious hinds the festive dance explore;
Their only wish (bland health and pleasure gay)
Th' Eternal grants—enraptur'd they adore!

Join then the blissful choir!—The chearful note
Let Echo's magic from the caves resound!

Whilst o'er the lawns astonish'd Wood-nymphs float,
And Sylphs, well-pleas'd, in myriads flock around!

Here if the poignant pangs of Sorrow dart,
Or the fell daemon Grief perchance alarms,
Safely repose each secret of thy heart,
And lull each care in Amarantha's arms!

Here too the spirit so completely blest
(A mother once—a guardian-angel now!)
Shall ease the sigh, which heaves thy labouring breast,
And heaven-ward waft the well-directed vow I

ELEGY XVIII.

THE

TEARS OF OLD MAR-DAY.

BY
EDWARD LOVETBOND, ESQ.

LED by the jocund train of vernal Hours
And vernal Airs, uprose the gentle May;
Blushing she rose, and blushing rose the flow'rs
That sprung spontaneous in the genial ray.

Her locks with heav'n's ambrosial dews were bright
And amorous Zephyrs flutter'd on her breast:
With ev'ry shifting gleam of morning light
The colors shifted of her rainbow vest.

Imperial ensigns grae'd her smiling form,

A golden key, and golden wand she bore ;
This charms to peace each sullen eastern storm,
And that unlocks the Summer's copious store.

Onward in conscious majesty she came,
The grateful honors of mankind to taste ;
To gather fairest wreaths of future fame,
And blend fresh triumphs with her glories past.

Vain hope! no more in choral bands unite
Her virgin vot'ries, and at early dawn,
Sacred to May and Love's mysterious rite,
Brush the light dew-drops from the spangled lawn.

To her no more Augusta's wealthy pride
Pours the full tribute from Potosi's mine ;
Nor fresh-blown garlands village maids provide,
A purer off'ring, at her rustie shrine.

No more the Maypole's verdant height around
To Valor's games th ambitious youth advance:
No merry bells and tabors' sprightlier sound
Wake the loud carol, and the sportive dance.

Sudden in pensive sadness droop'd her head,
Faint on her cheeks the blushing crimson dy'd
" O! chaste victorious triumphs, whither fled?
My maiden honors, whither gone ?" she cry'd.

Ah I once to fame and bright dominion born,
The Earth and smiling Ocean saw me rise,
With time coeval and the star of morn,
The first, the fairest daughter of the skies.

Then, when at heaven's prolific mandate sprung
The radiant beam of new-created day,
Celestial harps, to airs of triumph strung,
Hail'd the glad dawn, and angels call'd me MAY.

Space in her empty regions heard the sound,
And hills, and dales, and rocks, and valleys rung;
The sun exulted in his glorious round,
And shouting planets in their courses sung.

For. ever then I led the constant year;
Saw Youth, and Joy, and Love's enchanting wiles;
Saw the mild Graces in my train appear,
And infant Beauty brighten in my smiles.

No Winter frown'd. In sweet embrace ally'd,
Three sister Seasons danc'd th' eternal green;
And Spring's retiring softness gently vy'd
With Autumn's blush, and Summer's lofty mien.

Too soon, when man profan'd the blessings giv'n,
And vengeance arm'd to blot a guilty age,
With bright Astrea to my native heav'n
I fled, and flying saw the Deluge rage:

Saw bursting clouds eclipse the noontide beams,
While sounding billows from the mountains roll'd,
With bitter waves polluting all my streams,
My nectar'd streams, that flow'd on sands of gold.

Then vanish'd many a sea-girt isle and grove,
Their forests floating on the wat'ry plain :

Then fam'd for arts and laws deriv'd from Jove,
My Atalantis sunk beneath the main.

No longer bloom'd primeval Eden's bow'rs,
Nor guardian dragons watch'd th' Hesperian steep:
With all their fountains, fragrant fruits and flow'rs,
Torn from the continent to glut the deep.

No more to dwell in sylvan scenes I deign'd,
Yet oft descending to the languid earth,
With quick'ning pow'rs the fainting mass sustain'd,
And wak'd her slumb'ring atoms into birth,

And every echo caught my raptur'd name,
And every virgin breath'd heram'rous vows,
And precious wreaths of rich immortal fame,
Show'r'd by the Muses, crown'd my lofty brows.

But chief in Europe, and in Europe's pride,
My Albion's favor'd realms, I rose ador'd;
And pour'd my wealth, to other climes deny'd,
From Amalthea's horn with plenty stor'd.

Ah me ! for now a younger rival claims
My ravish'd honors, and to her belong
My choral dances, and victorious games,
To her my garlands and triumphal song.

O say what yet untasted bounties flow,
What purer joys await her gentle reign ?
Do lilies fairer, vi'lets sweeter blow ?
And warbles Philomel a softer strain ?

Do morning suns in ruddier glory rise?
Does ev'ning fan her with serener gales?
Do clouds drop fatness from the wealthier skies?
Or wantpns Plenty in her happier vales

Ah! no: the blunted beams of dawning light
Skirt the pale orient with uncertain day;
And Cynthia, riding on the car of night,
Through clouds embattled faintly wins her way.

Pale, immature, the blighted verdure springs,
Nor mounting juices feed the swelling flow'r;
Mute all the groves, nor Philomela sings
When silence listens at the midnight hour.

Nor wonder, man, that Nature's bashful face,
And op'ning charms her rude embraces fear:
Is she not sprung of April's wayward race,
The sickly daughter of th' unripen'd year?

With show'rs and sunshine in her fickle eyes,
With hollow smiles proclaiming treach'rous peace;
With blushes, harb'ring in their thin disguise
The blast that riots on the Spring's increase.

Is this the fair invested with my spoil
By Europe's laws, and Senates' stern command
Ungen'rous Europe, let me fly thy soil,
And waft my treasures to a grateful land:

Again revive on Asia's drooping shore
My Daphne's groves, or Lycia's ancient plain:
Again to Afric's sultry sands restore

Embow'ring shades, and Libyan Amnion's fane:

Or haste to northern Zembla's savage coast,
There hush to silence elemental strife;
Brood o'er the region of eternal Frost,
And swell her barren womb with heat and life.
Then Britain—here she ceas'd. Indignant grief, '
And parting pangs her fault'ring tongue supprest :
Veil'd in an amber cloud, she sought relief,
And tears, and silent anguish told the rest.

ELEGY XIX.

A
FAREWELL TO SUMMER.

ADIEU fair Spring 1 adorn'd with chaplets gay,
Ye fields and vernal landscapes all adieu,
Bright summer and the long transparent day,
No more I. hail the scented groves and you.

Farewell the walk where crystal rivulets glide,
Where slender osiers waft the healthful gale,
Where insects float along the silver tide,
And silent rapture haunts the fruitful vale.

Where purple lawns salubrious odors spread,
Where heath-shrubs blossom wild with languid dye,
Where round the hedge unbought perfumes are shed,
And native beauty courts the roving eye.

Where hawthorns bud, and velvet cowslips grow,
Where verdant banks put forth the painted weed,

Whose vivid hues eclipse th' embroider'd beau,
And the proud flaunters of the Park exceed.

Where Solitude unfolds her matchless charms,
And meek Content assumes her happy reign,
Where jocund Plenty crowns the rising farms,
And fills the storehouse of the village-swain.

How fresh past pleasures dance before the mind,
Renew'd in thought by winter's coming train,
That now, like vapors on the broad-wing'd wind,
Haste to deface the beauty of the plain.

I see, with memory's retrospective eye,
Each rivulet's polish'd current smoothly flow,
See blithsome May hang pearly blossoms high,
And richly dress the flowery meads below.

See nodding orchards wave their plumy pride,
See gardens grac'd with all the tints of spring,
Enamell'd beds their tender foliage hide,
Till genial suns a warmer season brin.

What scenes can equal summer's bright display,
When swift Aurora drives her early car,
When glowing Phoebus gives the blushing day,
And sends his boundless influence wide and far.

How sweet to see the flocks that crop their food,
And skip in wanton sport around the field,
Glad to present their bleating gratitude,
For the green pasture that the meadows yield.

To hear the wakeful shepherd's homely strain,
Breathe welcome sonnets to the rosy beam,
While slumbering towns in leaden sleep remain,
And lose substantial pleasures for a dream.

To tread betimes the neighbouring lanes, and view
(Ere scorching heat rides on the noon-tide air) "
The grass, the trees, the rallies rob'd in deir,
And garden plants the liquid garment wear.

There oft at morn I tun'd the rural lay,
And with my Sylvia gently stray'd along,
The birds sat mute on every leafy spray,
While listening echo catch'd the flowing song.

There silent mus'd on Shakspere's tragic page,
Of Milton learn'd to scale the azure road,
Chanted Maeonides' poetic rage,
And read, O Pope! thy equal thoughts of God.

Admhr'd great Thomson's active skilful muse,
That in such easy numbers scans the globe,
Such lively colors Albion's spring renews,
And paints the beauties of her vernal robe.

There, when the lark began her warbling song,
And shook her pinions for the morning flight,
Rais'd the loud chorus of the feather'd throng,
And tower'd beyond the farthest reach of sight.

The tuneful black-bird whistling to his mate,
Far o'er the lonely forest thrill'd the note,
And cheerful linnets in the woods, elate,

Rejoin'd the melting music of his throat.

Our praise reap'd fervor from the general glow,
The pious airs inspir'd the heavenly flame,
The thrush's plaint, the cattle's meaning low,
With grateful joy our swelling hearts o'ercame.

Nor less at eve the rural mansions please,
Or rgtral virtues charm th' exalted soul,
Whose powers not yet enervated by ease,
Like Newton, grasp creation's ample whole;

In search of learning's gifts unwearied roam,
Th' illumin'd spaces of the milky way,
Traverse th' infinitude of nature's dome,
The earth, its snow-top'd mountains, and the sea

In every part discover wisdom's hand,
Find Deity inscrib'd on all around,
Omnipotence and love from strand to strand,
Faas th' encircling ocean's utmost bound.

For such, O spring thy fragrant breezes blow,
Thy new-born flowers expand the crimson leaf;
Thy rays, O summer! golden prospects show,
And tinge the grain of Ceres' pointed sheaf.

For such, mild autumn rears the shooting vines,
Bids juicy clusters swarm the shaded wall,
Enriching crops o'erhang her wheaten mines
And ripen'd fruits from bending branches fall.

To such, e'en winter's jarring winds convey,

The gladsome tidings of eternal peace:
And storms and clouds, that others' bliss allay
Their hope, their strength, their fortitude increase.

ELEGY XX.

FOUR ELEGIES

BY JOHN SCOTT, ESQ

I. WRITTEN AT THE APPROACH OF SPRING.

STERN Winter hence with all his train removes;
And cheerful skies and limpid streams are seen;
Thick-sprouting foliage decorates the groves ;
Reviving herbage robes the fields in green,

Yet lovelier scenes shall crown th' advancing year,
When blooming Spring's full bounty is display'd ;
The smile of beauty every vale shall wear;
The voice of song enliven every shade.

O Fancy, paint not Coming days too fair!
Oft, for the prospects sprightly May should yieldsv
Rain-pouring clouds have darken'd all the air,
Or snows untimely whiten'd o'er the field:

But should kind Spring her wonted bounty shower,
The smile of beauty and the voice of song;
If gloomy thought the human mind o'erpower,
Ey'n vernal hours glide unenjoy'd along.

I shun the scenes where maddening Passion raves,

Where Pride and Folly high dominion hold,
And unrelenting Avarice drives her slaves
O'er prostrate Virtue in pursuit of gold :

The grassy lane, the wood-surrounded field,
The rude stone fence, with fragrant wall-flowers gay,
The clay-built cot, to me more pleasure yield
Than all the pomp imperial domes display ;

And yet ev'n here amid these secret shades,
These simple scenes of unreprov'd delight,
Affliction's iron hand my breast invades,
And Death's dread dart is ever in my sight.

While genial suns to genial showers succeed;
(The air all mildness, and the earth all bloom)
While herds and flocks range sportive o'er the mead,
Crop the sweet herb, and snuff the rich perfume;

O why alone to hapless man deny'd
To taste the bliss inferior beings boast!
O why this fate, that fear and pain divide —
His few short hours on earth's delightful coast!

Ah cease—no more of Providence complain
Tis sense of guilt that wakes the mind to woe,
Gives force to fear, adds energy to pain,
And palls each joy by heaven indulg'd below

Why else the smiling infant train so blest,
Ere dear-bought knowledge ends the peace within,
Or wild desire inflames the youthful breast,
Or ill propension ripens into sin ?

As to the bleating tenants of the field,
As to the sportive warblers on the trees,
To them their joys sincere their seasons yield,
And all their days and all their prospects please;

Such joys were mine when from the peopled streets,
Where on Thamesis' banks I liv'd immur'd,
The new blown fields that breath'd a thousand sweets,
To Surrey's wood-crown'd hills my steps allur'd:

O happy hours, beyond recovery fled!
What share I now, " that can your loss repay,"
While o'er my mind these glooms of thought are spread,
And veil the light of life's meridian ray ?

Is there no power this darkness to remove ?
The long-lost joys of Eden to restore ?
Or raise our views to happier seats above,
Where Fear, and Pain, and Death shall be no more

Yes, those there are who know a Saviour's love
The long lost joys of Eden can restore,
And raise their views to happier seats above,
Where Fear, and Pain, and Death shall be no more;

These grateful share the gift of Nature's hand
And in the varied scenes that round them shine,
(The Fair, the Rich, the Awful, and the Grand)
Admire th' amazing workmanship divine.

Blows not a flow'ret in th enamel'd vale,
Shines not a pebble where the riv'let stray;

Sports not an insect on the spicy gale,
But claims their wonder and excites their praise.

For them ev'n vernal nature looks more gay,
For them more lively hues the fields adorn ;
To them more fair the fairest smile of day, .
To them more sweet the sweetest breath of morn.

They feel the bliss that hope and faith supply:
They pass serene th' appointed hours that bring'
The day that wafts them to the realms on high,
The day that centers in eternal spring.

II. WRITTEN IN THE HOT WEATHER,

JULY, MDCCLVII.

By the Same.

THREE hours from noon the passing shadow shows,
The sultry breeze glides faintly o'er the plains ;
The dazzling aether fierce and fiercer glows,
And human nature scarce its rage sustains.

Now still and vacant is the dusty street, .
And still and vacant where yon fields extend,
Save where those swains, oppress'd with toil and heat,
The grassy harvest of the mead attend.

Lost is the lively aspect of the ground,
Low are the springs, the reedy ditches dry
No verdant spot in all the vale is found,
Save what yon stream's unfailing stores supply.

Where are the flowers that made the garden gay ?
Where is their beauty, where their fragrance fled ?
Their stems relax, fast fail their leaves away,
They fade and mingle with their dusty bed:

All but the natives of the torrid zone,
What Afric's wilds, or Peru's fields display,
Pleas'd with a clime that imitates their own,
They lovelier bloom beneath the parching ray

Where is wild nature's heart-reviving song,
That fill'd in genial Spring the verdant bowers ?
Silent in gloomy woods the feather'd throng
Pine through this long, long course of sultry hours.

Where is the dream of bliss by summer brought ?
The walk along the riv'let-water'd vale ?
The field with verdure clad, with fragrance fraught i
The sun mild-beaming, and the fanning gale

The weary soul Imagination chears,
Her pleasing colors paint the future gay ;
Time passes on, the truth itself appears,
The pleasing colors instant fade away :

In different seasons different joys we place,
And these shall Spring supply, and Summer these
Yet frequent storms the bloom of Spring deface,
And Summer scarcely brings a day to please.

O for some secret shady cool recess 1
Some Gothic dome o'erhung with darksome trees,

Where thick damp walls this raging heat repress;
Where the long isle invites the lazy breeze

Bat why these 'plaints?—Amid his wastes of sand,
Far more than this the wandering Arab feels;
Far more the Indian in Columbus' land,
While Phoebus o'er him rolls his fiery wheels:

Far more the sensible of mind sustains,
Rack'd with the poignant pangs of fear or shame;
The hopeless lover, bound in beauty's chains,
And he, whom envy robs of hard-earn'd fame:

He, who a father or a mother mourns,
Or lovely consort lost in early bloom;
He, whom the dreaded rage of fever burns,
Or slow disease leads lingering to the tomb.—

Lest man should sink beneath the present pain ;
Lest man should triumph in the present joy;
For him th' unvarying " Laws of heaven ordain,"
Hope in his ills, and to his bliss alloy.

Fierce and oppressive is the sun we share,
Yet not unuseful to our humid soil;
Hence shall our fruits a richer flavor bear,
Hence shall our plains with riper harvests smile:

Reflect, and be content—for mankind's good
Heaven gives the due degrees of drought or rain;
To-morrow ceaseless showers may swell the flood,
Nor soon yon sun rise blazing fierce again :

E'en now behold the grateful change at hand
Hark, in the east loud blustering gales aru
Wide and more wide the darkening clouds en
And distant light'nings flash along the skin

O in the awful concert of the storm,
While hail and rain, and wind and thunde
Let the great Ruler's praise my song inform,
Let wonder, reverence, gratitude be mine.

III. WRITTEN IN THE HARVEST.

FAREWELL the pleasant violet-scented shade;
The primros'd hill and daisy-mantled mead; -
The furrow'd land, with springing corn array'd;
The sunny wall, with bloomy branches spread.

Farewell the bower with blushing roses gay
Farewell the fragrant trefoil-purpled field ;
Farewell the walk through rows of new-mown hay,
When evening breezes mingled odors yield.

Farewell to these—now round the lonely farms,
Where jocund Plenty deigns to fix her seat;
Th' autumnal landscape opening all its charms,
Declares kind Nature's annual work complete.

In different parts what different views delight,
Where on neat ridges waves the golden grain;
Or where the bearded barley dazzling white,
Spreads o'er the steepy slope or wide champain.

The smile of Morning gleams along the hills;

And wakeful Labor calls her sons abroad;
They leave with cheerful look their lowly vills,
And bid the fields resign their ripen'd load.

To various tasks address the rustic band,
And here the scythe, and there the sickle wield ;
Or rear the new-bound sheaves along the land ;
Or range in heaps the produce of the field.

Some build the shocks, some load the spacious wains,
Some lead to sheltering barns the fragrant corn,
Some form tall ricks that tow'ring o'er the plains,
For many a mile the rural yards adorn.—

Th' inclosure gates thrown open all around,
The stubble's peopled by the gleaning throng,
The rattling car with verdant branches crown'd,
And joyful swains that raise the clamorous song,

Soon mark glad harvest o'er—Ye rural lords,
Whose wide domains o'er Albion's isle extend ;
Think whose kind hand your annual wealth affords,
And bid to heaven your grateful praise ascend.

For though no gift spontaneous of the ground
Rose these fair crops that made your vallies smile,
Though the blithe youth of every hamlet round
Pursued for these through many a day their toil;

Yet what avail your labors or your cares ?
Can all your labors, all your cares, supply
Bright suns, or softening showers, or tepid airs,
Or one indulgent influence of the sky ?

For Providence decrees that we obtain
With toil each blessing destin'd to our use;
But means to teach us that our toil is vain,
If he the bounty of his" hand refuse.

Yet, Albion, blame not what thy crime demands,
While this sad truth the blushing Muse betrays,
More frequent echoes o'er thy harvest lands
The voice of riot than the voice of praise.

Prolific though thy fields, and mild thy clime,
Know realms, once fam'd for fields and climes as fair,
Have fell the prey of famine, war, and time,
And now no semblance of their glory bear.

Ask Palestine, proud Asia's early boast,
Where now the groves that pour'd her wine and oil,
Where the fair towns that crown'd her wealthy coast,
Where the glad swains that till'd her fertile soil?

Ask, and behold, and mourn her hapless fall!
Where rose fair towns, where wav'd her golden grain,
Thron'd on the naked rock and mouldering wall,
Pale Want and Ruin hold their dreary reign.

Where Jordan's vallies smil'd in living green,
Where Sharon's flowers disclos'd their varied hues; |
The wandering pilgrim views the alter'd scene,
And drops the tear of pity as he views.

Ask Grecia, mourning o'er her ruin'd towers,
Where now the prospects charm'd her bards of old,

Her corn-clad mountains and Elysian bowers,
And silver streams through fragrant meadows roll'd?

Where Freedom's praise along the vale was heard,
And town to town return'd the favorite sound;
Where patriot War her awful standard rear'd
And brav'd the millions Persia pour'd around?

There Freedom's praise no more the valley chears,
There patriot War no more her banner waves;
Nor bard, nor sage, nor martial chief appears,
But stern Barbarians rule a land of slaves,

Of mighty realms are such the poor remains?
Of mighty realms that fell when mad with power,
They lur'd each vice to revel on their plains;
Each monster doom'd their offspring to devour I

O Albion! would'st thou shun their mournful fates,
To shun their follies and their crimes be thine;
And woo to linger in thy fair retreats,
The radiant virtues, progeny divine

Bright Truth, the noblest of the sacred band,
Sweet Peace whose brow no ruffling frown deforms,
Fair Charity with ever open hand,
And Courage smiling 'midst a thousand storms.

O haste to grace our isle, ye lovely train!
So may the Power whose hand all blessing yields,
Giye her fam'd glories ever to remain,
And crown with annual wealth her laughing fields.

IV. WRITTEN AT THE APPROACH OF WINTER.

By the Same.

THE sun far southward bends his annual way,
The bleak north-east wind lays the forest bare,
The fruit ungather'd quits the naked spray,
And dreary Winter reigns o'er earth and air.

No mark of vegetable life is seen,
No bird to bird repeats his tuneful call;
Save the dark leaves of some rude ever-green,
Save the lone red-breast on the moss-grown wall.

Where are the sprightly scenes by Spring supply'd,
The May-flower'd hedges scenting every beeez;
The white flocks scattering o'er the mountain side,
The woodlarks warbling on the blooming trees ?

Where is gay Summer's sportive insett train,
That in green fields on painted pinions play'd;
The herd at morn wide pasturing o'er the plain,
Or throng'd at noon-tide in the willow shade ?

Where is brown Autumn's evening mild and still,
What time the ripen'd corn fresh fragrance yields,
What time the village peoples all the hill,
And loud shouts echo o'er the harvest fields ?

To former scenes our fancy thus returns,
To former scenes that little pleas'd when here!
Our Winter chills us, and our Summer burns ;
Yet we dislike the changes of the year.

To happier lands then restless fancy flies,
Where Indian streams through green Savannahs flow;
Where brighter suns and ever tranquil skies
Bid new fruits ripen, and new flow'rets blow.

Let Truth these fairer happier lands survey,
There half the year descends in watery storms;
Or Nature sickens in the blaze of day,
And one brown hue the sun-burnt plain deforms.

There oft as toiling in the mazy fields,
Or homeward passing on the shadeless way,
His joyless life the weary labourer yields,
And instant drops beneath the deathful ray.

Who dreams of Nature free from Nature's strife ?
Who dreams of constant happiness below !
The hope-flush'd enterer on the stage of life;
The youth to knowledge unchastis'd by woe.

For me, long toil'd on many a weary road,
Led by false hope in search of many a joy ;
I find in earth's bleak clime no blest abode,
No place, no season sacred from annoy :

For me, while Winter rages round the plains,
With his dark days I'll human life compare:
Not those who fraught with clouds and winds and rains,
Than this with pining pain and anxious care.

O whence this wonderous turn of mind our fate !
Whate'er the season or the place possest,

We ever murmur at our present state,
And yet the thought of parting breaks our rest :

Why else, when heard in evening's solemn gloom,
Does the sad knell, that sounding o'er the plain
Tolls some poor lifeless body to the tomb,
Thus thrill my breast with melancholy pain ?

The voice of Reason echoes in my ear,
Thus thou ere long must join thy kindred clay ;
No more these " nostrils breathe the vital air,
" No more these eye-lids open on the day.

O Winter, round me spread thy joyless reign,
Thy threatening skies in dusky horrors drest ;
Of thy dread rage no longer I'll complain,
Nor ask an Eden for a transient guest.

Enough has heaven indulg'd of joy below,
To tempt our tarriance in this lov'd retreat;
Enough has heaven ordain'd of useful woe,
To make us languish for a happier seat.

There is, who deems all climes, all seasons fair,
There is, who knows no restless passion's strife;
Contentment smiling at each idle care ;
Contentment thankful for the gift of life;

She finds in Winter many a scene to please;
The morning landscape fring'd with frost-work ,
The sun at noon seen through the leafless trees.
The clear calm aether at the close of day :

She marks the advantage storms and clouds bestow,
When blustering Caums purifies the air,
When most Aquarius pours the fleecy snow,
That makes the impregnate glebe a richer harvest bear.

She bids for all our grateful praise arise,
To him whose mandate spake the world to form;
Gave Spring's gay bloom, and Summer's chearful skies,
And Autumn's corn-clad field, and Winter's sounding storm.

ELEGY XXI.

THE
PARTRIDGES.

WRITTEN ON THE LAST OF AUGUST.

BY THE REV. MR. PRATT.

HARD by yon copse, that skirts the flowery vale,
As late I walk'd to taste the evening breeze,
A plaintive murmur mingled in the gale,
And notes of sorrow echo'd through the trees.

Touch'd by the pensive sound, I nearer drew
But my rude step increas'd the cause of pain :
Soon o'er my head the whirring Partridge flew,
Alarm'd ; and with her flew an infant train.

But short the excursion ;—for, unus'd to play,
Feebly the unfledg'd wings th' essay could make:
The parent, shelter'd by the closing day,
Lodg'd her lov'd covey in a neighb'ring brake.

Her cradling pinions there she amply spread,
And hush'd th' affrighted family to rest;
But still the late alarm suggested dread,
And closer to their feathery friend they press'd.

She, wretched parent! doom'd to various woe,
Felt all a mother's hope, a mother's care;
With grief foresaw the dawn's impending blow,
And to avert it thus preferr'd her prayer:

O thou! who e'en the sparrow dost befriend,
Whose providence protects the harmless wren;
Thou God of birds! these innocents defend,
From the vile sport of unrelenting men.

For soon as dawn shall dapple yonder skies,
The slaught'ring gunner, with the tube of fate,
While the dire dog the faithless stubble tries
Shall persecute our tribe with annual hate.

O may the sun, unfann'd by cooling gale,
Parch with unusual heat th' undewy ground;
So shall the pointer's wonted cunning fail,
So shall the sportsman leave my babes unfound.

Then shall I fearless guide them to the mead,
Then shall I see with joy their plumage grow;
Then shall I see (fond thought!) their future breed,
And every transport of a parent know.

But if some victim must endure the dart,
And Fate marks out that victim from my race,

Strike, strike the eaden vengeance through this heart;
Spare, spare my babes; and I the death embrace.

ELEGY XXII.

THE GOLDFINCHES.

BY THE REV. RICHARD JAGO, M.A.

—Ingenuaa didicisse fideliter arte
Emollit mores, nec sinit esse feros.

To you, whose groves protect the feather'd quires,
Who lend their artless notes a willing ear,
To you, whom pity moves, and taste inspires,
The Doric strain belongs; O Shenstone, hear.

'Twas gentle spring, when all the tuneful race,
By nature taught, in nuptial leagues combine:
A goldfinch joy'd to meet the warm embrace,
And hearts and fortunes with her mate to join,

Through Nature's spacious walks at large they rang'd,
No settled haunts, no fix'd abode their aim;
As chance or fancy led, their path they chang'd,
Themselves, in every vary'd scene, the same.

Till on a day to weighty cares resign'd,
With mutual choice, alternate they agreed,
On rambling thoughts no more to turn their mind,
But settle soberly, and raise a breed.

All in a garden, on a currant-bush,
With wond'rous art they built their waving seat,
In the next orchard liv'd a friendly thrush,
Not distant far, a woodlark's soft retreat,

Here blest with ease, and in each other blest,
With early songs they wak'd the sprightly groves,
'Till time matur'd their bliss, and crown'd their nest
With infant pledges of their faithful loves.

And now what transport glow'd in either's eye!
What equal fondness dealt th' allotted food!
What joy each other's likeness to descry,
And future sonnets in the chirping brood !

But ah! what earthly happiness can last ?
How does the fairest purpose often fail ?
A truant school-boy's wantonness could blast
Their rising hopes, and leave them both to wail.

The most ungentle of his tribe was he ;
No gen'rous precept ever touch'd his heart:
With concords false and hideous prosody
He scrawl'd his task, and blunder'd o'er his part.

On barb'rous plunder bent, with savage eye
He mark'd where wrapt in down the younglings lay,
Then rushing seiz'd the wretched family,
And bore them in his impious hands away.

But how shall I relate in numbers rude
The pangs for poor Chrysomitris decreed

When from a neighb'ring spray aghast she view'd
The savage ruffian's inauspicious deed!

So, wrapt in grief, some heart-struck matron stands,
While horrid flame surround her children's room !
On heav'n she calls, and wrings her trembling hands,
Constrain'd to see, but not prevent their doom.

" O grief of griefs! with shrieking voice she cry'd,
What sight is this that I have liv'd to see ?
O that 1 had a maiden-goldfinch died,
From love's false joys, and bitter sorrows free!

" Was it for this, alas! with weary bill,
Was it for this, I pois'd th' unwieldy straw
For this I pick'd the moss from yonder hill ?
Nor shun'd the pond'rous chat along to draw ?

" Was it for this, I cull'd the wool with care;
And strove with all my skill our work to crown ?
For this, with pain I bent the stubborn hair;
And lin'd our cradle with the thistle's down ?

" Was it for this my freedom I resign'd ;
. And ceas'd to rove from beauteous plain to plain ?
For this I sat at home whole days confin'd,
And bore the scorching heat, and pealing rain i

 Was it for this my watchful eyes grow dim
The crimson roses on my cheek turn pale ?
Pale is my golden plumage, once so trim ;
And all my wonted spirits 'gin to fail.

" O plund'rer vile; O more than weezel fell!
More treach'rous than the cat with prudish face?
More fierce than kites with whom the furies dwell !
More pilf'ring than the cuckow's prowling race!

" For thee may plumb or goosb'ry never grow,
Nor juicy currant cool thy clammy throat:
But bloody birch-twigs work thee shameful woe,—
Nor ever goldfinch cheer thee with her note !"

Thus sang the mournful bird her piteous tale,
The piteous tale her mournful mate return'd:
Then side by side they sought the distant vale,
And there in silent sadness inly mourn'd.

ELEGY XXIII.

THE
BLACKBIRDS.

By the Same,

THE sun had chas'd the mountain snow,
And kindly loos'd the frozen soil,
The melting streams began to flow,
And ploughmen urg'd their annual toil.

'Twas then, amid the vocal throng
Whom nature wakes to mirth and love,
A blackbird rais'd his am'rous song,
And thus it echo'd through the grove.

O fairest of the feather'd train!

For whom I sing, for whom I burn.
Attend with pity to my strain,
And grant my love a kind return.

For see the wintry storms are flown,
And gently Zephyrs fan the air;
Let us the genial influence own, .
Let us the vernal pastime share.

-The raven plumes his jetty wing
To please his croaking paramour ;
The larks responsive ditties sing,
And tell their passion as they soar.

But trust me, love, the raven's wing
Is not to be compar'd with mine;
Nor can the lark so sweetly sing
As I, who strength with sweetness join.

O! let me all thy steps attend
I'll point new treasures to thy sight;
Whether the grove thy wish befriend,
Or hedge-rows green, or meadows bright.

I'll shew my love the clearest rill
Whose streams among the pebbles stray:
These will we sip, and sip our fill,
Or on the flow'ry margin play.

I'll lead her to the thickest brake,
Impervious to the school-boy's eye;
For her the plaister'd nest I'll make,
And on her downy pinions lie.

When, prompted by a mother's care,
Her warmth shall form th' imprison'd young;
The pleasing task I'll gladly share,
Or cheer her labors with my song.

To bring her food I'll range the fields,
And cull the best of every kind;
Whatever nature's bounty yields,
And love's assiduous care can find.

And when my lovely mate would stray
To taste the summer sweets at large,
I'll wait at home the live-long day,
And tend with care our little charge.'

Then prove with me the sweets of love,
With me divide the cares of life;
No bush shall boast in all the grove
So fond a mate, so blest a wife.

He ceas'd his song. The melting dame
With soft indulgence heard the strain
She felt, she own'd a mutual flame,
And hasted to relieve his pain.

He led her to the nuptial bower,
And nestled closely to her side ;
The fondest bridegroom of that hour,
And she, the most delighted bride.

Next morn he wak'd her with a song,
" Behold, he said, the new-born day

The lark his matin peal has rung,
Arise, my love, and come away."

Together through the fields they stray'd.
And to the murm'ring riv'let's side ;
Renew'd their vows, and hopp'd and play'd,
With honest joy and decent pride.

When oh! with grief the Muse relates
The mournful sequel of my talc ;
Sent by an order from the fates,
A gunner met them in the vale.

Alarm'd, the lover cry'd, My dear,
Haste, haste away, from danger fly ;
Here, gunner, point thy thunder herc;
O spare my love, and let me die.

At him the gunner took his aim;
His aim, alas! was all too true:
O ! had he chose some other game
Or shot—as he was wont to do

Divided pair! forgive the wrong,
While I with tears your fate rehearse ;
I'll join the widow's plaintive song,
And save the lover in my verse.

ELEGY XXIV.

THE

SWALLOWS.

WRITTEN SEPTEMBER, MDCCXLVIII.

IN TWO PARTS,

By the Same,

ERE yellow Autumn from our plains retir'd,
And gave to wintry storms the varied year,
The Swallow-race, with foresight clear inspir'd,
To Southern climes prepar'd their course to steer.

On ***Damon's*** roofs a grave assembly sate;
His roof, a refuge to the feather'd kind;
With serious look he mark'd the nice debate,
And to his ***Delia*** thus address'd his mind.

Observe yon twitt'ring flock, my gentle maid,
Observe, and read the wondrous ways of heav'n
With us through summer's genial reign they stay'd,
And food and lodging to their wants were giv'n.

But now, through sacred prescience, well they know
The near approach of elemental strife;
The blustry tempest, and the chilling snow,
With every want and scourge of tender life!

Thus taught, they meditate a speedy flight;
For this ev'n now they prune their vig'rous wing;
For this consult, advise, prepare, excite,
And prove their strength in many an airy ring

No sorrow loads their breast, or swells their eye,
To quit their friendly haunts, or native home;
Nor fear they, launching on the boundless sky,
In search of future settlements to roam.

They feel a pow'r, an impulse all divine !
 That warns them hence; they feel it, and obey;
To this direction all their cares resign,
Unknown their destin'd stage, unmark'd their way.

Well fare your flight! ye mild domestic race
Oh! for your wings to travel with the sun
Health brace your nerves, and Zephyrs aid your pace,
'Till your long voyage happily be done!

See, **Delia**, on my roof your guests to day;
To-morrow on my roof your guests no more !
Ere yet 'tis night, with haste they wing away,
To morrow lands them on some safer shore.

How just the moral in this scene convey'd!
And what without a moral would we read ?
Then mark what **Damon** tells his gentle maid,
And with ***his*** lesson register the deed.

Tis thus life's chearful seasons roll away ;
Thus threats the winter of inclement age ;

Our time of action but a summer's day;
And earth's frail orb the sadly-varied stage!

And does no pow'r its friendly aid dispense,
Nor give *us* tidings of some happier clime ?
Find *we* no guide in gracious Providence
Beyond the stroke of death, the verge of time ?

Yes, yes, the sacred oracles we hear,
That point the path to realms of endless day ;
That bid our hearts, nor death, nor anguish fear,
This future transport, *that* to life the way.

Then let us timely for our flight prepare,
And form the soul for her divine abode;
Obey the call, and trust the Leader's care
To bring us safe through Virtue's paths to God.

Let no fond love for earth exact: a sigh,
No doubts divert our steady steps aside;
Nor let us long to live, nor dread to die;
Heav'n is our Hope, and Providence our Guide

PART II.

WRITTEN APRIL, MDCCXLIX.

AT length the winter's surly blasts are o'er ;
Array'd in smiles the lovely spring returns:
Health to the breeze unbars the screaming door,
And every breast with heat celestial burns.

Again the daisies peep, the violets blow ; .

Again the tenants of the leafy grove,
Forgot the patt'ring hail, the driving snow,
Resume the lay to melody and love.

And see, my Delia, see o'er yonder stream,
Where on the sunny bank the lambkins play;
Alike attracted to th' enliv'ning gleam,
The stranger-swallows take their wonted way.

Welcome, ye gentle tribe, your sports pursue,
Welcome again to Delia, and to me :
Your peaceful councils on my roof renew,
And plan your settlements from danger free.

No tempest on my shed its fury pours,
My frugal hearth no noxious blast supplies;
Go, wand'rers, go, repair your sooty bow'rs,
Think, on no hostile roof my chimnies rise.

Again I'll listen to your grave debates,
I'll think I hear your various maxims told,
Your numbers, leaders, politics, and states,
Your limits settled, and your tribes enroll'd.

I'll think I hear you tell of distant lands,
What insect-nations rise from Egypt's mud,
What painted swarms subsist on Libya's sands,
What mild Euphrates yields, and Ganges' flood.

Thrice happy race! whom Nature's call invites
To travel o'er her realms with active wing,
To taste her choicest stores, her best delights,
The summer's radiance, and the sweets of spring:

While we are doom'd to bear the restless change
Of shifting seasons, vapors dank, or dry,
Forbid, like you, to milder climes to range,
When wintry clouds deform the troubled sky.

But know the period to your joys assign'd !
Know ruin hovers o'er this earthly ball;
Certain as fate, and sudden as the wind,
Its secret adamantine props shall fall.

Yet when your short-liv'd summers shine no more,
My patient mind, sworn foe to vice's way,
Sustain'd on lighter wings than yours, shall soar
To fairer realms beneath a brighter ray ;

To plains etherial, and Elysian bowers,
Where wintry storms no rude access obtain,
Where blasts no light'ning, and no thunder low'rs,
But spring and joy unchanged for ever reign.

ELEGY XXV.

WRITTEN ON

VALENTINE MORNING.

BY THE HON.

HORACE WALPOLE.

HARK, through the sacred silence of the night,
Loud Chanticleer doth sound his clarion shrill,

Hailing with song the first pale gleam of light,
That floats the dark brow of yon eastern hill.

Bright star of morn, oh! leave not yet the wave,
To deck the dewy frontlet of the day,
Nor thou, Aurora, quit Tithonus' cave,
Nor drive retiring darkness yet away,

Ere these my rustic hands a garland twine,
Ere yet my tongue indite a simple song,
For her I mean to hail my Valentine,
Sweet maiden, fairest of the virgin throng.

Sweet is the morn, and sweet the gentle breeze
That fans the fragrant bosom of the spring,
Sweet chirps the lark, and sweeter far than these
The gentle love-song gurgling turtles sing.

Oh let the flowers be fragrant as the morn
And as the turtle's song my ditty sweet:
Those flowers my woven chaplet must adorn,
That ditty must my waking charmer greet.

And thou, blest saint, whom choral creatures join
In one enlivening symphony to hail,
Oh be propitious, gentle Valentine,
And let each holy tender sigh prevail.

Oh give me to approach my sleeping love,
And strew her pillow with the freshest flowers,
No sigh unhallow'd shall my bosom move,
Nor step prophane pollute my true-love's bowers.

At sacred distance only will I gaze,
Nor bid my unreproved eye refrain,
Mean while my tongue shall chaunt her beauty's praise,
And hail her sleeping with the gentlest strain.

Awake my fair, awake, for it is time;
Hark, thousand songsters rise from yonder grove,
And rising carol this sweet hour of prime,
Each to his mate, a roundelay of love.

All nature sings the hymeneal song,
All nature follows, where the spring invites;
Come forth, my love, to us these joys belong,
Ours is the spring, and all her young delights,

For us she throws profusely forth her flowers,
Which in fresh chaplets joyful I will twine;
Come forth, my fair, oh do not lose these hours,
But wake, and be my faithful Valentine.

Full many an hour, all lonely have I sigh'd,
Nor dared the secret of my love reveal,
Full many a fond expedient have I tried
My warmest wish in silence to conceal.

And oft to far retired solitude
All mournfully my slow step have I bent,
Luxurious there indulg'd my musing mood,
And there alone have given my sorrows vent.

This day resolv'd I dare to plight my vow,
This day, long since the feast of love decreed,
Embolden'd will I speak my flame, nor thou .

Refuse to hear how sore my heart does bleed.

Yet if I should behold my love awake,
Ah, frail resolves, ah whither will ye fly?
Full well I know I shall not silence break,
But struck with awe almost for fear shall die.

Oh no, I will not trust a fault'ring speech
In broken phrase an awkward tale to tell
A tale, whose tenderness no tongue can reach,
Nor softest melody can utter well.

But my meek eye, best herald to my heart,
I will compose to soft and downcast look,
And at one humble glance it shall impart
My love, nor fear the language be mistook.

For she shall read (apt scholar at this lore)
With what fond passion my true bosom glows.
How hopeless of return I still adore,
Nor dare the boldness of my wish disclose.

Should she then smile,—yet ah! she smiles on all,
Her gentle temper pities all distress;
On every hill, each vale, the sun-beams fall,
Each herb, and flower, each tree, and shrub the bless.

Alike all nature grateful owns the boon,
The universal ray to all is free ;
Like fond Endymion should I hope the moon,
Because among the rest she shines on me?

Hope, vain presumer, keep, oh keep away:

Ev'n if my woe her gentle bosom move,
Pity some look of kindness may display;
But each soft glance is not a look of love.

Yet, heav'nly visitant, thou dost not quit
Those bow'rs where angels sweet division sing,
Nor deignest thou on mortal shrine to sit,
Alone, for round thee ever on the wing,

Glad choirs of love, attend, and hov'ring wait
Thy mild command; of these thy blooming train
Oh bid some sylph in morning dreams relate,
Ere yet my love awake, my secret pain.

ELEGY XXVI.

BY

ROBERT LLOYD, M. A.

A MONTH hath roll'd its lazy hours away,
Since Delia's presence bless'd her longing swain;
How could he brook the sluggish Time's delay,
What charm could soften such an age of pain?

One fond reflection still his bosom chear'd,
And sooth'd the torments of a lover's care,
Twas that for Delia's self the bower he rear'd,
And fancy plac'd the nymph already there,

O come, dear maid, and, with a gentle smile,
Such as lights up my lovely fair-one's face,
Survey the product of thy shepherd's toil,

Nor rob the villa of the villa's grace.

Whate'er improvements strike thy curious sight,
Thy taste hath form'd—let me not call it mine,
Since, when I muse on thee, and feed delight,
I form no thought that is not wholly thine.

TV apartments destin'd for my charmer's use,
(For love in trifles is conspicuous shown)
Can scarce an object to thy view produce,
But bears the dear resemblance of thine own.

And trust me, love, I could almost believe
This little spot the mansion of my fair;
But that awak'd from fancy's dreams, I grieve
To find its proper owner is not there,

Oh! I could doat upon the rural scene,
Its prospect over hill and champaign wide,
But that it marks the tedious way between,
That parts thy Damon from his promis'd brid.

The gardens now put forth their blossoms sweet,
In Nature's flowery mantle gaily drest,
The close-trimm'd hedge, and circling border neat,
All ask my Delia for their dearest guest.

The lily pale, the purple blushing rose,
In this fair spot their mingled beauties join ;
The woodbine here its curling tendrils throws,
In wreaths fantastic, round the mantling vine.

The branching arbor here, for lovers made,

For dalliance meet, or song, or amorous tale,
Shall oft protect us with its cooling shade,
When sultry Phoebus burns the lowly vale.

'Tis all another paradise around;
And, trust me, so it would appear to me,
Like the first man were I not lonely found,!
And but half blest, my Delia, wanting thee.

For two, but two, I've form'd a lovely walk,
And I have call'd it by my fair-one's name;
Here, blest with thee, t' enjoy thy pleasing talk,
While fools and madmen bow the knee to fame.

The rustic path already have I try'd,
Oft at the sinking of the setting day;
And while, my love, I thought thee by my side,
With careful steps have worn its edge away.

With thee I' ve held discourse, how passing sweet
While fancy brought thee to my raptur'd dream;
With thee have prattled in my lone retreat,
And talk'd down suns on love's delicious theme.

Oft, as I wander through the rustic crowd,
Musing with downcast look, and folded arms,
They stare with wonder when I rave aloud,
And dwell with rapture on thy artless charms,

They call me mad, and oft with finger rude,
Point at me leering, as I heedless pass;
Yet Colin knows the cause, for love is shrewd,
And the young shepherd courts the farmer's lass.

Among the fruits that grace this little seat,
And all around their clustering foliage spread,
Here mayst thou cull the peach, or nectarine sweet,
And pluck the strawberry from its native bed.

And all along the river's verdant side,
I' ve planted elms, which rise in even row,
And fling their lofty branches far and wide,
Which float reflected in the lake below.

Since I've been absent from my lovely fair,
Imagination forms a thousand schemes;
For O! my Delia, thou art all my care,
And all with me is love and golden dreams.

O flattering promise of secure delight!
When will the lazy-pacing hours be o'er,
That I may fly with rapture to thy sight,
And we shall meet again to part no more?

ELEGY XXVII.

THE WISH.

TO

URANIA.

BY THOMAS BLACKLOCK, D. D.

LET others travel, with incessant pain,
The wealth of earth and ocean to secure ;

Then with fond hopes caress the precious bane;
In grandeur abject, and in affluence poor.

But soon, too soon, in Fancy's timid eyes,
Wild waves shall roll, and conflagrations spread;
While bright in arms, and of gigantic size,
The fear-form'd robber haunts the thorny bed,

Let me, in dreadless poverty retir'd,
The real joys of life, unenvied, share:
Favour'd by Love, and by the Muse inspir'd,
I'll yield to wealth its jealousy and care.

On rising ground, the prospect to command,
Unting'd with smoke, where vernal breezes blow,
In rural neatness let my cottage stand;
Here wave a wood, and there a river flow.

Oft from the neighbouring hills and pastures round,
Let sheep with tender bleat salute my ear;
Nor fox insidious haunt the guiltless ground,
Nor man pursue the trade of murder near

Far hence, kind heaven expel the savage train,
Inur'd to blood, and eager to destroy;
Who pointed steel with recent slaughter stain,
And place in groans and death their cruel joy.

Ye Powers of social life and tender song
To you devoted shall my fields remain;
Here undisturb'd the peaceful day prolong,
Nor own a smart but Love's delightful pain.

For you, my trees shall wave their leafy shade;
For you, my gardens tinge the lenient air;
For you, be Autumn's blushing gifts display'd,
And all that Nature yields of sweet or fair.

But, O! if plaints which love and grief inspire,
In heavenly breasts could e'er compassion find,
Grant me, ah! grant my heart's supreme desire,
And teach my dear Urania to be kind.

For her, black Sadness clouds my brightest day;
For her, in tears the midnight vigils roll:
For her, cold horrors melt my powers away,
And chill the living vigor of my soul

Beneath her scorn each youthful ardor dies,
Its joys, its wishes, and its hopes, expire
In vain the fields of Science tempt my eyes :
In vain for me the Muses string the lyre.

O! let her oft my humble dwelling grace,
Humble no more, if there she deign to shine;
For heaven, unlimited by time or place,
Still waits on god-like worth and charms divine

Amid the cooling fragrance of the morn,
How sweet with her through lonely fields to stray
Her charms the loveliest land skip shall adorn,
And add new glories to the rising day.

With her, all Nature shines in heighten'd bloom;
The silver stream in sweeter music flows;
Odors more rich the fanning gales perfume;

And deeper tinctures paint the spreading rose.

With her, the shades of night their horrors lose,
Its deepest silence charms if she be by;
Her voice the music of the dawn renews,
Its lambent radiance sparkles in her eye.

How sweet, with her, in Wisdom's calm recess,
To brighten soft desire with wit refin'd!
Kind Nature's laws with sacred Ashley trace,
And view the fairest features of the mind!

Or borne on Milton's flight, as heaven sublime,
View its full blaze in open prospect glow;
Bless the first pair in Eden's happy clime,
Or drop the human tear for endless woe.

And when, in virtue, and in peace grown old,
No arts the languid lamp of life restore:
Her let me grasp with hands convuls'd and cold,
Till every nerve relax'd can hold no more.

Long, long on her my dying eyes suspend,
Till the last beam shall vibrate on my sight;
Then soar where only greater joys attend,
And bear her image to eternal light.

Fond man, ah! whither would thy fancy rove?
Tis thine to languish in unpitied smart;
Tis thine, alas! eternal scorn to prove,
Nor feel one gleam of comfort warm thy heart.

But, if my fair this cruel law impose,

Pleas'd, to her will I all my soul resign;
To walk beneath the burden of my woes,
Or sink in death, nor at my fate repine.

Yet when, with woes unmingled and sincere
To Earth's cold womb in silence I descend:
Let her, to grace my obsequies, appear,
And with the weeping throng her sorrows blend.

Ah! no, be all her hours with pleasure crown'd,
And all her soul from every anguish free :
Should my sad fate that gentle bosom wound,
The joys of heaven would be no joys to me.

ELEGY XXVIII.

CONJUGAL LOVE.

BY THE REV. S. HENLEY.

But happy they! the happiest of their kind I
Whom gentler stars unite, and in one fate
Their hearts, their fortunes, and their beings blend.
Thomson.

IF aught of genuine bliss hath e'er been giv'n,
To those that dwell so far beneath the skies,
That bliss which constitutes on earth an heav'n,
Can only from the purest passion rise.

" Say, do not storms uproot|the lofty oak,
That crowns with majesty the mountain's brow;
While lowly shrubs escape the thunder's stroke,

And wave their verdure in the vale below ?

Say, does that soil whose bosom gold contains,
From its rich lap in more profusion throw,
Or, sweeter flow'rsthan scent unpillag'd plains,
Where baneful gold hath ne'er been taught to glow ?

Say, does that haughty bird, whose gaudy train
Attracts the full gaze of the splendid day,
Pour from the heart so soothing, sweet a strain,
As modest Philomela's melting lay ?

Ambition, av'rice, and the pomp of pride,
Seductive, oft may lure unheedful eyes,
But ne'er will tempt my devious steps aside ;
These, who pursue will ne'er obtain the prize.

Remote from envy, far from madding strife,
I nothing want, of competence possess'd;
Amid the scenes of mild domestic life,
I'll seek, by blessing others, to be blest.

Mine be the first, the most endearing care,
That nought may e'er disturb my DELIA'S joy;
Whate'er could cause to her the lightest fear,
Would, instant, all my happiness destroy.

For her I'd wake, soon as the gleam of morn,
And, blithsome, at the heavy plough would toil;
Anticipating, e'er my wish'd return,
The ready welcome of a heart-felt smile.

When harvest o'er my field its produce spreads,

And vying reapers bend in adverse rows;
With pleasure she the yellow landscape treads,
And wipes the sweat of labor from their brows.

Should sickness e'er molest my menial train,
With lenient hand she'd ev'ry grief asswage;
Her sympathy would draw the sting of pain,
Revive the young, and charm e'en wayward age.

Should some kind friend enter my humble shed,
With studious ease she'd grace the frugal board;
Before her guest our rural treasures spread,
Nor boast a treat but what our fields afford.

Should some bewilder'd trav'ller as he strays,
For shelter seek beneath our lonely roof,
She makes for him the cheerful hearth to blaze;
Of hospitality the readiest proof!

The warmest raptures of the bridal bed,
When first entrans'd we seal'd our mutual vow,
With less delight the thrilling breast o'erspread,
Than the fond bliss we both experience now.

Ah, speak, my Delia, thy o'erflowing heart,
When cradled in thine arm the tender boy
First, with a filial smile begins t' impart
He knows his mother, source of all his joy.

Or, when around my knees the infant band,
In clamb'ring contest seek the envi'd kiss;
When struggling each extends the eager hand,
To plead his claim, and all obtain the bliss :

While we in fond contention, strive to trace,
In which, each parent's semblance most prevails;
Their father's vigor and thy winning grace,
In varied mixture o'er each feature steals.

Oft when their fait'ring tongue but ill can tell
The little fancies in their brain that rise, "
With pleas'd attention thou explor'st them well,
And read'st their meaning, in their speaking eyes.

" Delightful task! the tender thought to rear,
To teach the young idea how to shoot;"
To prune each impulse that a vice might bear,
Or tend with fost'ring hand the rip'ning fruit

When tott'ring lambkins, from the searching air,
Unable yet the fresh world to sustain,
Require the shed; be theirs the trembling care,
Nor will they let the suff'rers bleat in vain.

" When timid red-breasts, pinch'd by taming cold,
Visit our friendly cot in search of food,
Be their's the joy to make the strangers bold,
And learn the luxury of doing good.

Thus, with their op'ning minds our pleasures spread,
While they in all that's just and gen'rous thrive;
Till autumn's mellowing hue our days o'ershade,
Then in our scyons, we'll again revive,

Fond mem'ry then will make us feel anew,
Those happy hours when you first touch'd my heart;

Recall each soft endearment to our view,
When you, who wounded, smiling, eas'd the smart.

Then, in my boys, some lovely maid I'll woo,
Whose virtues and whose form resemble thine;
While, in your girls, shall pay his court to you,
Some honest youth, whose bosom throbs like mine.

And when, at last, draws on the gloom of death,
We'll thank our GOD for all his blessings giv'n;
To gentle slumber yield our easy breath,
And, both transported wake to bliss in heav'n.

ELEGY XXIX.

IL LATTE. BY EDWARD JERNINGHAM, ESQ.

incipe, parve puer, risu cognncocere matrctr.

YE fair, for whom the hands of HYMEN weave
The nuptial wreath to deck your virgin brow,
While pleasing pains the conscious bosom heave,
And on the kindling cheek the blushes glow :

Whose spotless soul contains the better dow'r,
Whose life unstain'd full many virtues vouch,
For whom now Venus frames the fragrant bow'r,
And scatters roses o'er the destin'd couch:

To you I sing.—Ah 1 ere the raptur'd youth
With trembling hand removes the jealous veil,
Where, long regardless of the vows of truth,
Unsocial coyness stamp'd th' ungrateful seal:

Allow the poet round your flowing hair,
Cull'd from an humble vale, a wreath to twine,
To Beauty's altar with the loves repair,
And wake the lute beside that living shrine :

That sacred shrine! where female virtue glows,
To which retreat the warm affections fly ;
Where Love is born, where strong attachment g
Where frames pure Constancy the faithful tye

That shrine! where Nature with presaging aim,
What time her friendly aid Luc IN A brings,
The snowy nectar pours, delightful stream
Where flutt'ring Cupids dip their purple wing

For you who bear a Mother's sacred name,
Whose cradled offspring, in lamenting strain,
With artless eloquence asserts his claim,
The boon of Nature, but asserts in vain :

Say why, illustrious daughters of the Great,
Lives not the nursling at your tender breast
By you protefted in his frail estate ?
By you attended, and by you caress'd ?

To venal hands, alas 1 can you resign
The Parent's task, the Mother's pleasing care i
To venal hands the smiling babe consign ?
While HYMEN starts, and Nature drops a tear.

When 'mid the polish'd circle ye rejoice,
Or roving join fantastic Pleasure's train,

Unheard perchance the nursling lifts his voice,
His tears unnotic'd, and unsooth'd his pain.

Ah ! what avails the coral crown'd with gold
In heedless infancy the title vain ?
The colors gay the purfled scarfs unfold ?
The splendid nurs'ry, and th' attendant train !

Far better hadst thou first beheld the light
Beneath the rafter of some roof obscure;
There in a Mother's eye to read delight,
And in her cradling arm repose secure.

Nor wonder, should HYGEIA, blissful Queen!
Her wonted salutary gifts recall,
While haggard Pain applies his dagger keen,
And o'er the cradle Death unfolds his pall,

The flow'ret ravish'd from its native air,
And bid to flourish in a foreign vale,
Does it not oft elude the planter's care,
And breathe its dying odors on the gale ?

For you, ye plighted fair, when Hymen crowns
With tender offspring your unshaken love,
Behold them not with Rigor's chilling frowns,
Nor from your sight unfeelingly remove.,

Unsway'd by Fashion's dull unseemly jest,
Still to the bosom let your infant cling,
There banquet oft, an ever-welcome guest,
Unblam'd inebriate at that healthful spring.

With fond solicitude each pain assuage,
Explain the look, awake the ready smile;
Unfeign'd attachment so shall you engage,
To crown with gratitude maternal toil:

So shall your daughters, in Affliction's day,
When o'er your form the gloom of age shall spread,
With lenient converse chase the hours away,
And smooth with Duty's hand the widow'd bed:

Approach, compassionate, the voice of Grief,
And whisper patience to the closing ear;
From Comfort's chalice minister relief,
And in the potion drop a filial tear.

So shall your sons, when beauty's charms are fled,
When fades the languid lustre in your eye;
When Flattery shuns her Hybla-drops to shed,
The want of beauty, and of praise, supply :

E'en from the wreath that decks the warrior's brow,
Some chosen leaves your peaceful walks shall strew
And e'en the flow'rs on classic ground, that blow,
Shall all unfold their choicest sweets for you.

When to th' embattled host the trumpet blows,
While at the call fair ALBION'S gallant train
Dare to the field their triple-number'd foes,
And chase them speeding o'er the martial plain:

The mother kindles at the glorious thought,
And to her son's renown adjojns her name ;
For at the nurt' ring breast the **Hero** caught

The love of Virtue, and the love of Fame.

Or in the senate, when Britannia's cause
With gen'rous themes inspires the glowjng mind,
While list'ning Freedom grateful looks applause,
Pale Slav'ry drops her chain, and sculks behind:

With conscious joy the tender parent fraught,
Still to her son's renown adjoins her name;
For at the nurt'ring breast the **Patriot** caught
The love of Virtue, and the love of Fame :

Yet then, ascending still with bolder view,
Should the blest youth to heav'nly gifts aspire,
While with keen eye he pierces nature through,
The flame of Genius sets his soul on fire:

The Mother yields to Glory's soaring thought,
And arts of thrilling transport touch her frame ;
For at the nurt'ring breast the **Pott** caught
The love of Virtue, and the love of Fame.

ELEGY XXX.

DELIA.

BY MRS. BARBAULD.

———-tecum ut longae sociarem gaudia yitae,
Inque tuo caderet nostra senecta sinu. Tibul.

YES, DELIA loves! My fondest vows are blest;

Farewell the memory of her past disdain;
One kind relenting glance has heal'd my breast,
And balanc'd in a moment years of pain.

O'er her soft cheek consenting blushes move,
And with kind stealth her secret soul betray;
Blushes, which usher in the morn of love,
Sure as the red'ning east foretels the day.

Her tender smiles shall pay me with delight
For many a bitter pang of jealous fear;
For many an anxious day, and sleepless night,
For many a stifled sigh, and silent tear.

DELIA shall come, and bless my lone retreat;
She does not scorn the shepherd's lowly life;
She will not blush to leave the splendid seat,
And own the title of a poor man's wife.

he simple knot shall bind her gather'd hair,
The russet garment clasp her lovely breast:
DELIA shall mix amongst the rural fair,
By charms alone distinguish'd from the rest.

And meek Simplicity, neglected maid,
Shall bid my fair in native graces shine :
She, only she, shall lend her modest aid,
Chaste, sober priestess, at sweet beauty's shrine !

How sweet to muse by murmuring springs reclin'd;
Or loitering careless in the shady grove,
Indulge the gentlest feelings of the mind,
And pity those who live to aught but love!

When DELIA'S hand unlocks her shining hair,
And o'er her shoulder spreads the flowing gold
Base were the man who one bright tress would spare
For all the ore of India's coarser mold.

By her dear side with what content I'd toil,
Patient of any labor in her sight;
Guide the slow plough, or turn the stubborn soil,
Till the last, ling'ring beam of doubtful light.

But softer tasks divide my DELIA'S hours;
To watch the firstlings at their harmless play;
With welcome shade to screen the languid flowers,
That sicken in the summer's parching ray,

Oft will she stoop amidst her evening walk,
With tender hand each bruised plant to rear;
To bind the drooping lily's broken stalk,
And nurse the blossoms of the infant year.

When beating rains forbid our feet to roam,
We'll shelter'd sit, and turn the storied page:
There see what passions shake the lofty dome
With mad ambition or ungovern'd rage :

What headlong ruin oft involves the great;
What conscious terrors guilty bosoms proves;
What strange and sudden turns of adverse fate
Tear the sad virgin from her plighted love.

DELIA shall read, and drop a gentle tear;
Then cast her eyes around the low-roof'd cot,

And own the fates have dealt more kindly here,
That bless'd with only love our little lot.

For love has sworn (I heard the awful vow)
The wav'ring heart shall never be his care,
That stoops at any baser shrine to bow;
And what he cannot rule, he scorns to share.

My heart in DELIA is so fully blest,
It has no room to lodge another joy;
My peace all leans upon that gentle breast,
And only there misfortune can annoy.

Our silent hours shall steal unmark'd away
In one long tender calm of rural peace;
And measure many a fair unblemish'd day
Of cheerful leisure and poetic ease.

The proud unfeeling world their lot shall scorn
Who 'midst inglorious shades can poorly dwell:
Yet if some youth, for gentler passions born,
Shall chance to wander near our lowly cell,

His feeling breast with purer flame shall glow;
And leaving pomp, and state, and cares behind,
Shall own the world has little to bestow
Where two fond hearts in equal love are join'd.

ELEGY XXX.

CYNTHIA.

BY THE RIGHT RET.

THOMAS PERCY, D. D.

[Lord Bishopof Dromore.]

Libeat tibi Cynthia mecum
Roacida muscosis antra tenere jugis.   Propert.

BENEATH an aged oak's embow'ring shade,
Whose spreading arms with gray moss fringed were,
Around whose trunk the clasping stray'd;
A love-lorn youth oft pensive would repair.

' Fast by, a Naiade taught her stream to glide,
Which through the dale a winding channel wore:
The silver willow deck'd its verdant side,
[The whisp'ring sedges wav'd along the shore

Here oft, when Morn peep'd o'er the dusky hill;
Here oft, whenEvc bedew'd the misty vale;
Careless he laid him all beside the rill,
And pour'd in strains like these his attics tale.

Ah would he say—and then a sigh would heave:
Ah, Cynthia! sweeter than the breath of morn,
Soft as the gentle breath that fans at eve,

Of thee bereft, how shall I live forlorn?

Ah! what avails this sweetly solemn bow'r,
That silent stream where dimpling eddies play;
Yon thymy bank bedeck'd with many a flow'r,
Where maple-tufts exclude the beam of day?

Robb'd of my love, for how can these delight,
Though lavish Spring her smiles around has cast 1
Despair, alas! that whelms the soul in night,
Dims the sad eye and deadens every taste.

As droops the lily at the blighting gale;
Or crimson-spotted cowslip of the mead,
Whose tender stalk (alas 1 their stalk so frail)
Some hasty foot hath bruis'd with heedless tread:

As droops the woodbine, when some village hind
Hath fell'd the sappling elm it fondly bound;
No more it gadding dances in the wind,
But trails its fading beauties on the ground:

So droops my soul, dear maid, downcast, and sad,
For ever ah 1 for ever torn from thee;
Bereft of each sweet hope, which once it had,
When love, when treacherous love first smil'doome.

Return, blest days, return, ye laughing hours,
Which led me up the roseat steep of youth;
Which strew'd my simple path with vernal flow'rs,
And bade me court chaste Science and fair Truth.

Ye know, the curling breeze, oi gilded fly

That idly wantons in the noon-tide air,
Was not so free, was not so gay as I,
For ah ! I knew not then or love, or care.

Witness, ye winged daughters of the year,
If e'er a sigh had learnt to heave my breast
If e'er my cheek was conscious of a tear,
'Till Cynthia came and robb'd my soul of rest!

O have you seen, bath'd in the morning dew,
The budding rose its infant bloom display;
When first its virgin tints unfold to view,
It shrinks and scarcely trusts the blaze of day ?

So soft, so delicate, so sweet she came,
Youth's damask glow just dawning on her cheek:
I gaz'd, I sigh'd, I caught the tender flame,
Felt the fond pang, and droop'd with passion, weak

Yet not unpitied was my pain the while;
For oft beside yon sweet-briar in the dale,
With many a blush, with many a melting smile,
She sate and listen'd to the plaintive tale.

Ah me ! I fondly dreamt of pleasures rare,
Nor deem'd so sweet a face with scorn could glow;
How could you cruel then pronounce despair,
Chill the warm hope, and plant the thorn of woe?

What though no treasure canker in my chest,
Nor crowds of suppliant vassals hail me lord !
What though my roof can boast no princely guest,
Nor surfeits lurk beneath my frugal board 1

Yet should Content, that shuns the gilded bed,
With smiling Peace, and Virtue there forgot,[shed,
And rose-lip'd Health, which haunts the straw-built
With cherub Joy, frequent my little cot:

Led by chaste Love, the decent band should come,
O charmer would'st thou deign my roof to share!
Nor should the Muses scorn our simple dome,
Or knit in mystic dance the Graces fair.

The woodland nymphs, and gentle fays, at eve
Forth from the dripping cave and mossy dell,
Should round our hearth fantastic measures weave,
And shield from mischief by their guardian spell.

Come then, bright maid, and quit the city throng;
Have rural joys no charm to win the soul ? —
She proud, alas! derides my lowly song,
Scorns the fond vow, and spurns the russet stole.

Then, Love, begone, thy thriftless empire yield,
In youthful toils I'll lose th' unmanly pain:
With echoing horns I'll rouse the jocund field,
Urge the keen chace, and sweep along the plain.

Or all in some lone moss-rown tow'r sublime,
With midnight lamp I'll watch pale Cynthia round,
Explore the choicest rolls of ancient Time,
And heal with Wisdom's balm my hapless wound,

Or else I'll roam—Ah no! that sigh profound
Tells me that stubborn love disdains to yield ;

Nor flight, nor Wisdom's balm can heal the wound,
Nor pain forsake me in the jocund field.

ELEGY XXXII.

DAMON AND SYLVIA.

AH me! that restless bliss so soon should flie!
Still as think my yielding maid to gain,
And flatt'ring hope says all my joys are nigh,
Officious jealousy renews my pain.

When cold suspense and torturing despair,
When pausing doubt, and anxious fear's no more,
Some idle falshood haunts my list'ning ear,
And wakes my heart to all it felt before.

One treads the mazes of the puzzled dance
With easy step, and unaffected air,
False rapture feigns, or rolls a meaning glance,
To catch the open, easy-hearted fair.

Another boasts a more substantial claim,
For him fair Plenty fills her golden horn,
A thousand flocks support his haughty flame,
A thousand acres crown'd with waving corn.

But I nor tread the mazes of the dance
With easy step, and unaffected air,
Nor rapture feign, nor roll a meaning glance,
To catch the open, easy-hearted fair.

I boast not Fortune's more substantial claim,

For me nor Plenty fills her golden horn,
Nor wealthy flocks support my humble flame,
Nor smiling acres crown'd with waving corn.

Say, will thy gen'rous heart for these reject
A tender passion, and a soul sincere?
For though with me you've little to expect,
Believe me, Sylvia, you have less to fear.

Come, let us tread the flow'ry paths of peace,
'Till Fate shall seal th' irrevocable doom;
Then soar together to yon realms of bliss,
And leave our mingled ashes in the tomb.

Perhaps some tender sympathetic breast,
Who knows with Sorrow's elegance to moan,
May search the charnel where our relics rest,
And grave our mem'ry on the faithful stone.

" Tread soft, ye lovers, o'er this hallow 'd ground
Here lies fond Damon by his Sylvia's side;
Their souls in life by mutual love were bound,
Nor death the lasting union could divide."

ELEGY XXXIII.

TO

DAMON.

No longer hope, fond youth, to hide thy pain,
No longer blush the secret to impart;
Too well I know what broken murmurs mean,

And sighs that burst, half stifled, from the heart.

Nor did I learn this skill by Ovid's rule,
The magic arts are to thy friend unknown:
I never studied but in Myra's school,
And only judge thy passion by my own.

Believe me, Love is jealous of his power;
Confess betimes the influence of the God,
The stubborn feel new torments every hour;
To merit mercy we must kiss the rod.

In vain, alas! you seek the lonely grove,
And in sad numbers to the Thames complain;
The shade with kindred softness sooths thy love,
Sad numbers sooth, but cannot cure, thy pain.

When Phoebus felt (as story sings) the smart,
By the coy beauties of his Daphne fir'd,
Not Phoebus' self could profit by his art,
Tho' all the Nine the sacred lay inspir'd.

Even should the maid vouchsafe to hear thy song,
No tender feelings will its sorrows raise ;
For verse hath mourn'd imagin'd woes so long,
She'll hear unmov'd, and, without pitying, praise.

Nor yet proud maid, shouldst thou refuse thin ,ear,
Nor are the manners of the poet rude,
Nor pours he not the sympathetic tear,
His heart by anguish, not his own, subdued.

When fairest names in long oblivion rot,

(For fairest names must yield to wasting time,
The poet's mistress 'scapes the common lot,
And blooms uninjur'd in his living rhime.

ELEGY XXXIV.

ANSWER

TO THE

FOREGOING.

" Warm from the soul, and faithful to its fires."   Pope.

THOU, whom long since I number'd for my own,
To whose kind view in life's first happy days
Each young ambition of my heart was known,
For fame my ardor, and my love of ease,

Say, wilt thou pardon, that awhile I thought
(The thought how vain !) my feelings to disguise \
Too well thou knew'st, by Myra's lessons taught,
The soul's soft language, and the voice of eyes:

Thou knew'st—perhaps, ere to myself 'twas known—
The impatient struggling of the sigh supprest:
And early saw'st, instructed by thy own,
The infant passion kindling in my breast:

" No longer then I'll seek to hide my pain,
No longer blush the secret to impart;"
The mask which wrong'd thy friendship, I disdain,
" And boast the graceful weakness of my heart."

Nor shall the jealous God with hand severe
Afflict his vassal, tho' a rebel long;
Already hath he breath'd the humble prayer,
And pour'd already the repentant song,

But, ah! in vain his art the poet tries,
The power of numbers he exerts in vain ;
The maid regards them with unconscious eyes,
And hears, but will not understand, the strain :

Yet hath she seen—for nothing could conceal—
The wild emotions of his labouring breast;
The fond attention, that devour'd her tale;
The hand that trembled, when her hand it prest:

While his pleas'd ear upon her accents hung,
Oft hath she mark'd the involuntary sigh,
Love's "broken murmurs" forming on his tongue,
And love's warm rapture starting to his eye :

And she hath seen him whelm'd in bitterest woe,
When her frown spoke some error unforgiven;
And she hath seen each kindling feature glow,
When her smile cheer'd him with a gleam of heaven.

But, when in verse he breathes his amorous care,
(As if she knew not what to all is known)
His arts she praises, but neglects his prayer,
Nor deem the poet, or the verse, her own.

Say then, O say (for, sure, thou know'st full well
Each tender thought with happiest skill to dress)

His heart's strong feelings how his tongue shall tell!
How speak—what language never can express

Teach him those arts that did thy suit commend
When love first prompted Myra to be kind;
And, that those arts may prosper, let thy friend
His love's soft advocate in Myra find.

Then, while the happy means thy lesson shows
To win the maid his passion to approve,
Then Myra shall recount—for Myra knows—
What blessings are in store for those that love:

Myra shall tell her, that from love alone
Flows the pure spring of happiness sincere;
And love, with power to lovers only known,
Doubles each joy, and lessens every care ;

And each warm transport of her conscious heart,
And each fair hope, that doth her state attend,
With generous ardor Myra shall impart,
And point her own example to her friend :

And if her sense shall Damon's claim approve,
And if her candor deem his vow sincere,
Her tongue shall speak the interest of his love,
Her gentle eloquence enforce his prayer:

And all that tenderest pity can suggest,
And each soft argument her thought can find,
Myra shall urge—O be her pleading blest !—
To win her fair companion to be kind:

And when—for friendship must not pass them o'er—
She gives the frailties of his youth to sight,
O may her pencil place—he asks no more—
Each little merit in the fairest light!

Clara, perchance, may learn to love an heart,
(Proud tho' the boast, it is an honest pride)
Where nothing selfish ever claim'd a part,
Which owns no purpose it should wish to hide;

Warm with the love of virtue and mankind,
At others bliss where social feelings glow;
And where, when sorrow wrings the worthy mind,
The tear is ready for another's woe:

This praise the youth is fond to call his own;
No higher worth he seeks his claim to grace;
His hope he builds upon his love alone,
And his love stands on reason's solid base :

No sudden blaze, the meteor of a day,
Its transient splendor o'er his heart doth pour;
Kindled at virtue's fire, the steady ray
Shall shine thro' life, and gild its latest hour.

If such an heart can please, if such a flame
With kindred ardor can inspire her breast,
His first ambition hath obtain'd its aim
To Heaven and Fortune he commits the rest.

But, if regardless of the honest prayer,
The maid unpitying, on his love should frown;
If fate's worst shock the youth is doom'd to bear,

Each prospect darken'd, and each hope o'er thrown;

Too humbly fearful of th' all-ruling power
To strike the blow that sets the spirit free,
Prison'd in life, he'll wait the appointed hour,
And, patient, bend him to the hard decree:

Yet ne'er (however shifts the varying scene)
Shall her dear image from his mind depart;
Still fresh'd the lov'd idea shall remain,
Warm in each pulse, and woven with his heart:

Unchang'd thro' life, still anxious for her peace,
For her to heaven his daily prayer shall rise;
And, when kind fate shall grant the wish'd release,
His last weak breath shall bless her as it flies :

Then, when in earth's cold womb his limbs are laid,
(For, sure, her servant's fall shall reach her ear)
Clara, perchance, will sigh, and grant his shade
The kind compassion of a pious tear:

Yes—she will weep—for gentle is her breast
Tho' his love pleas'd not, she will mourn his doom;
And, haply, when with flowers his grave is drest,
Her hand may plant a myrtle o'er his tomb.

This meed, at least, his service may demand ;
This—and 'tis all he asks—his truth may claim:
No breathing marble o'er his dust shall stand ;
No storied urn shall celebrate his name :

Enough for him, that, where his ashes lie,

When kindred spirits shall at times repair,
The prosperous youth shall cast a pitying eye,
The slighted virgin pour her sorrows there :

Enough for him, that pointing to his stone,
The sad old man his story shall relate,
Then smite his breast, and wish, with many a groan,
No child of his may meet so hard a fate.

ELEGY XXXV.

TWO

LOVE ELEGIES.

'Tis night, dead night; and o'er the plain
Darkness extends her ebon ray,
While wide along the gloomy scene Deep
Silence holds her solemn sway:

Throughout the earth no chearful beam
The melancholic eye surveys,
Save where the worm's fantastic gleam
The 'nighted traveller betrays:

The savage race (so Heaven decrees)
No longer through the forest rove ;
All nature rests, and not a breeze
Disturbs the stillness of the grove:

All nature rests; in Sleep's soft arms
The village swain forgets his care :
Sleep that the sting of Sorrow charms,

And heals all sadness but Despair;

Despair alone her power denies,
And when the sun withdraws his rays,
To the wild beach distracted flies,
Or cheerless through the desart strays;

Or to the church-yard's horrors led,
While fearful echoes burst around,
On some cold stone he leans his head,
Or throws his body on the ground.

To some such drear and solemn scene,
Some friendly power direct my way,
Where pale Misfortune's haggard train,
Sad luxury! delight to stray.

Wrapp'd in the solitary gloom,
Retir'd from life's fantastic crew,
Resign'd I'll wait my final doom,
And bid the busy world adieu.

The world has now no joy for me,
Nor can life now one pleasure boast,
Since all my eyes desir'd to see, —
My wish, my hope, my all, is lost;

Since she, so form'd to please and bless,
So wise, so innocent, so fair,
Whose converse sweet made sorrow lesss,
And brighten'd ail the gloom of care:

Since she is lost,—Ye powers divine,

What have I done, or thought, or said,
O say, what horrid ct of mine
Has drawn this vengeance on my head?

Why should Heaven favour Lycon's claim!
Why are my heart's best wishes crost?
What fairer deeds adorn his name?
What nobler merit can he boast?

What higher worth in him was found
My true heart's service to outweigh
A senseless fop!—A dull compound
Of scarcely animated clay

He dress'd, indeed, he danc'd with ease,
And charm'd her by repeating o'er
Unmeaning raptures in her praise,
That twenty fools had said before:

But I, alas! who thought all art
My passion's force would meanly prove,
Could only boast an honest heart,
And claim'd no merit but my love.

Have I not sate—Ye conscious hours
Be witness—while my Stella sang,
From morn to eve, with all my powers
Rapt in th' enchantment of hex tongue?

Ye conscious hours, that saw me stand
Entranc'd in wonder and surprise,
In silent rapture press her hand,
With passion bursting from my eyes,

Have I not lov'd—O earth and heaven
Where now is all my youthful boast
The dear exchange I hop'd was given
For slighted fame and fortune lost

Where now the joys that once were mine
Where all my hopes of future bliss?
Must I those joys, these hopes resign?
Is all her friendship come to this }

Must then each woman faithless prove,
And each fond lover be undone?
Are vows no more!—Almighty Love
The sad resemblance let me shun!

It will not be   My honest heart
The dear sad image still retains;
And, spite of reason, spite of art,
The dreadful memory remains.

Ye powers divine, whose wond'rous skill
Deep in the womb of time can see,
Behold, I bend me to your will,
Nor dare arraign your high decree.

Let her be blest with health, with ease,
With all your bounty has in store;
Let sorrow cloud my future days,
Be Stella blest 1—I ask no more.

But lo! where, high in yonder East,
The star of morning mounts apace 1

Hence !—let me fly th' unwelcome guest,
And bid the Muse's labor cease.

ELEGY THE SECOND.

WHEN young, life's journey I began,
The glittering prospect charm'd my eyes;
I saw along th' extended plan
Joy after joy successive rise:

And Fame her golden trumpet blew;
And Power display'd her gorgeous charms ;
And wealth engag'd my wandering view ;
And Pleasure woo'd me to her arms :

To each by turns my vows I paid,
As Folly led me to admire ;
While Fancy magnified each shade,
And Hope increas'd each fond desire:

But soon I found 'twas all a dream ;
And learn'd the fond pursuit to shun,
Where few can reach their purpos'd aim
And thousands daily are undone :

And Fame, I found, was empty air;
And Wealth had Terror for her guest;
And Pleasure's path was strewn with Care;
And Power was vanity at best.

Tir'd of the chace, I gave it o'er;
And, in a far sequester'd shade,
To Contemplation's sober power

My youth's next services I paid.

There Health and Peace adorned the scene;
And oft, indulgent to my prayer,
With mirthful eye and frolic mien,
The Muse would deign to visit there:

There would she oft delighted rove
The flower-enamel'd vale along;
Or wander with me through the grove,
And listen to the woodlark's song:

Or, 'mid the forest's awful gloom,
While wild amazement fill'd my eyes,
Recall past ages from the tomb,
And bid ideal worlds arise.

Thus in the Muse's favor blest,
One wish alone my soul could frame,
And Heaven bestow'd, to crown the rest,
A friend, and Thyrsis was his name.

For manly constancy and truth,
And worth unconscious of a stain,
He bloom'd the flower of Britain's youth,
The boast and wonder of the plain.

Still with our years our friendship grew;
No cares did then my peace destroy ;
Time brought new blessings as he flew,
And every hour was wing'd with joy.

But soon the blissful scene was lost,

Soon did the sad reverse appear;
Love came, like an untimely frost,
To blast the promise of my year.

I saw young Daphne's angel-form,
(Fool that I was, I bless'd the smart)
And, while I gaz'd, nor thought of harm.
The dear infection seiz'd my heart.

She was—at least in Damon's eyes—
Made up of loveliness and grace,
Her heart a stranger to disguise,
Her mind as perfect as her face;

To hear her speak, to see her move,
(Unhappy I, alas 1 the while)
Her voice was joy, her look was love,
And Heaven was open'd in her smile 1

She heard me breathe my amorous prayers, '
She listen'd to the tender strain,
She heard my sighs, she saw my tears,
And seem'd at length to share my pain :

She said she lov'd—and I, poor youth !
(How soon, alas, can Hope persuade !
Thought all she said no more than truth,
And all my love was well repaid.

In jcys, unknown to courts or kings,
With her I sat the live-long day,
And said and look'd such tender things,
As none beside could look or say !

How soon can Fortune shift the scene,
And all our earthly bliss destroy ?
Care hovers round, and Grief's fell train
Still treads upon the heels of Joy.

My age's hope, my youth's best boast,
My soul's chief blessing, and my pride,
In one sad moment all were lost,
And Daphne chang'd, and Thyrsis died.

O who, that heard her vows ere-while,
Could dream these vows were insincere ?
Or who could think, that saw her smile,
That faud could find admittance there

Yet she was false—my heart will break
Her frauds, her perjuries were such
Some other tongue than mine must speak
I have not power to say how much !

Ye swains, hence warn'd, avoid the bait,
O shun her paths, the traitress shun !
Her voice is death, her smile is fate,
Who hears, or sees her, is undone.

And, when Death's hand shall close my eye,
(For soon I know, the day will come)
O chear my spirit with a sigh,
And grave these lines upon my tomb

THE EPITAPH.

CONSIGN'D to dust, beneath this stone,
In manhood's prime is Damon laid;
Joyless he liv'd, and dy'd unknown
In bleak misfortune's barren shade.

Lov'd by the Muse, but lov'd in vain
Twas beauty drew his ruin on;
He saw young Daphne on the plain;
He lov'd, believ'd, and was undone.

His heart then sunk beneath the storm,
(Sad meed of unexampled truth)
And sorrow, like an envious worm,
Devour'd the blossom of his youth. -

Beneath this stone the youth is laid—
O greet his ashes with a tear !
May Heaven with blessings crown his shade,
And grant that peace he wanted here !

NOTES

ON

ELEGIES

MORAL, DESCRIPTIVE, AND AMATORY.

ELEGY I.

Page 1. THE ingenious and amiable Author of this and the subsequent Elegies, was the son of a Baker at Cambridge, and born in the beginning of the year 1714-15 in the parish of St. Botolph. From some ordinary school in the place of his nativity, he was removed to Winchester, through the favor of Mr. Bromley, father of Lord Montfort. At this seminary he cultivated his poetical talents, and with such success as to attract the notice of Pope. He was school-tutor to the father of the present Lord Portsmouth, and for sometime enjoyed the office of pre-positor, but unfortunately and unfairly, lost his election. ' His father having died before this disappointment, he, soon after, removed to Cambridge; and being the orphan of a baker, was admitted sizar of Clare-Hall, on a scholarship founded by Mr. pyke, who had been of that trade. The notice taken of him while at Winchester by Mr. Pope, and his own amiable manners, conspired to introduce him into college with eclat, and he soon formed an intimacy with some of the most respectable amongst his contemporaries in Cambridge, which continued unbroken thro' life : in this list the names of Powell, Balguy, and Hurd may be given. The first, however, of his productions, which in the opinion of Mr. Mason, intitled him a Poet, was his " Epistle on the danger of writing Verse." His " Essay on Ridicule'9 next followed, and shortly after his " Epistle on Nobility," inscribed to the Earl of Ashburnham, who, with the late Charles Townshend, was a student at Clare-Hall, and both honored him with their friendship. Though the latter, mixing in the busy world, had his attention withdrawn from our Poet, yet in respect to his other connexions he was not so unfortunate: whilst Mr. Wright and Mr. Saunderson, two clergy men, in particular realised the regard they professed. To the former Mr. Whitehead addressed several of his poems, and to the latter, the elegy with the coin of Aurelius. After having continued in college to the year 1742, in a manner highly reputable to him self, he was elected fellow, and purposed to enter into orders, when fortunately Commissary Graves re commended him to the late Earl of Jersey, as tutor to his son. In this situation, Mr. Whitehead relinquished his former plan, and having more time than official occupation, began to write for the stage. His first production was the *"Roman Father,"* which met with considerable applause. " Creusa" followed, but with less of success, though certainly a better Composition. It being now determined that Lord Villiers should travel, and that Lord Nuneham, his friend, should be of the party, Mr. Whitehead was appointed governor to both. In treading on the embers of classic remains, it can scarcely be imagined that the foot of the Muse should be inconscious of their glow; accordingly the "*Elegy at Haut-Vil-Iters*, with the others which follow, were the result of this excursion. Whilst in Italy, the office of secretary and register of the order of the Bath, becoming vacant, was procured for Mr. Whitehead by the intervention of Lady Jersey; and about two years after, on the death of Cibber, the laureat followed without solicitation. Returning to England, Mr. Whitehead had so well satisfied by his conduct the parents of his pupils, that he was solicited to live in the family of Lord Jersey, and to consider Lord Har-court's, as even his home. With the former he took up his abode, and continued in his house for fourteen years together. In this recess his "*School for Lovers*" was written, and brought on the stage in the year 1762. In the same year was produced also his "*Charge to the Poets,*" which drew on him the resentment of Churchill in his "*Rosciad.*" About this period, he amused himself with sketching out a farce, which being intended to exhibit Mrs. Clive in a new point of view, was exhibited in the year 1770 under the title of the "*Trip to Scotland.*" This producion, Mr. Mason declares, the only thing of 1 the kind that can be put in competition with the *petites pieces* " of Man Vaux. Besides "*Variety,*" the "*Goa's Beard*" and some other little poems, Mr. Whitehead revived his theatric ideas, and it appears from his Memoirs by Mr. Mason, that a com-pleat tragedy, with other dramatic remains are still in the hands of his friends.—" Here concluding his literary history," says his elegant Biographer, " I have nothing to add respecting his life, except what relates to its final close, at his lodgings in Charles-Street, Grosvenor-Square, April 14, 1785, which happily for himself, as it must be for all who pass through this world in the same blameless manner, with the same confidence in their God, and belief in his re-vealed will, so to die," was sudden, and without a groan.

ELEGY II.

Page 5. The Mausoleum of Augustus is now a garden belonging to Marchese di Corre.

6. *And the first rites to gloomy Dis convey'd.*] He is said to have been the first person buried in this monument.

ibid. Witness thou Field of Mars, that oft hadst known]

Quantos ille virum magnam Mavortis ad urbem
Campus aget gemitus !

6. ***Witness thou Tuscan stream, where oft he glow'd***]

—Vel quae, Tyberine, vidcbis
Funera, cum tumulum praeterlabere rccentem !
VIRG.

ELEGY IV.

Page 12. Whilst o'er yon hill, th' exalted Trophy shows] The trophies of Marius, now erected before the Capitol.

ELEGY V.

Page 15. ***'Twas in this isle,***] The insula Tiberina, where there are still some small remains of the famous temple of Aesculapius.

ELEGY VI.

Page 18. ***Behold my Friend, to this small orb confin'd***] The medal of Marcus Aurelius.

ELEGY VII.

Page 21. ***When St. John's name illumin'd Glory's page?***] Alluding to this couplet of Mr. Pope's.

To CATO Virgil paid one honest line,

O let my country's friends *illumine* mine.

23. ***For trust, with reverence trust this Sabine strain:***]
—Dignum laude Virum
Musa vctat mori. Hon A C R.

ELEGY VIll.

Page* 24. *My mimic reed first tun'd the Dorian Lay,] MUSAEUS, the first Poem in Mr. Mason's Collection, written while the Author was a scholar of St. John's College in Cambridge.

26. ***Mild as the fabled Form that whilom deign' d,***
At Milton's call, in Harefield's haunts to rove.] See the Description of the Genius of the Wood, in MILTON'S Arcades.

For know, by lot, from Jove, I am the Power
Of this fair wood, and live in oaken bower;
To nurse the Saplings tall, and curl the grove
With ringlets quaint, &c.

ELEGY IX.

***Page* 29.** This Elegy was prefixt to the former editions of CARACTACUS, as dedicatory of that Poem.

31. ***Her cheap applauses to the Susy stage,***
And leave him pensive Virtue's silent tear:-

Nil equidem feci (tu scis hoc ipse) Theatris; Musa nee in plausus ambitiosa mca est.
OVID. Trist. Lib. V. El. vii.23.

32. *"See from his mother earth God's blessings spring,* "*And eat his bread in peace and privacy.*"] Verbatim from a letter of HOOKER'S to Archbishop WHITGIFT. " But, my Lord, I shall never be able to finish what I have begun, [viz. his immortal Treatise on Ecclesiastical Polity] unless I be removed into some quiet country parsonage, *where I may see God's blessings spring out of my mother earth, and eat my own bread in peace and privacy,* " See his Life in the Bio-graphia Britannica.

ELEGY X,

page 33. Dr. Langhorne was a native of Kirby-Stephen in the county of Westmoreland, and the son of a clergyman. Being sent to Cambridge for his education, and having taken orders, he became tutor to a son of Mr. Cracroft of Lincolnshire, and afterward married his daughter. This Lady soon dying, he remained not long a widower. By his second marriage he had a daughter, whom, her mother being no more, he consigned at his death to the care of Mrs. Edridge, at that time Miss Gil man.

ELEGY XIV.

Page 54. *See Charles, more pleas'd, within the convent gloom.*] Charles V. of Spain, who in the zenith of his glory relinquished the throne to his son Philip, and retired to a convent in Estremadura.

ELEGY XV.

Page. 59. *Even he, sole terror of a venal age.*] Mr. Pope.

ibid. He too, who " mounts and keeps his distant way ,"] Mr. Gray.

ELEGY XVIII.

Page 69. *Brush the light dew-drops from the spangled lawn.'*] Alluding to the country custom of gathering May-dew.

ibid. To her no more Augusta's wealthy pride
Pours the full tribute from Potosi's mine ;
Nor fresh-blown garlands village maids provide,
A purer off' ering, at her rustic shrine.,]

The plate garlands of London. 70.

My Atalantis sunk beneath the main.] See Plato.

ELEGY XX.

Page 79. The Author of these Elegies, and many other poetic compositions, was a quaker, much re-spedled for his liberality and beloved for his worth.

ELEGY XXII,

Page- 99. The Author of this, and some subsequent Elegies, was Vicar of Snittersfield in Warwickshire. and Rector of Kimcote in Leicestershire. From his school days he was the intimate friend and correspondent of Shenstone. Having completed his education at University-College, Oxford, he took his degree of M. A. in 1738, and died in 1781.

101. *The pangs for poor Chrysomitris decreed!"*]
Chrysomitris, it seems, is the name for a goldfinch.

ELEGY XXX.

Page 142. *Or crimson-spotted cowslip of the mead,"*]
—On her left breast
A mole cinque-spotted : like the crimson drops
I* th' bottom of a cowslip.

SHAKSPERE'S Cymbeline, Act 3.

ELEGY XXXIII.

Page 149. ***No longer hope, fond youth, to hide thy pain,***]

Non ego celari possim, quid nutus amantis,
Quidve ferantmiti lenia verba sono.
Nee mihi sunt fortes.   TIBULL.

ibid. Confess betimes the influence of the God,]

Desine dissimulare 5 Deus crudeliusurit.
Quos videt invitos succubuisse sibi.   TIBULL.

www.bookjungle.com *email: sales@bookjungle.com fax: 630-214-0564 mail: Book Jungle PO Box 2226 Champaign, IL 61825*

The Codes Of Hammurabi And Moses
W. W. Davies

QTY

The discovery of the Hammurabi Code is one of the greatest achievements of archaeology, and is of paramount interest, not only to the student of the Bible, but also to all those interested in ancient history...

Religion   ISBN: *1-59462-338-4*   Pages:132
MSRP *$12.95*

The Theory of Moral Sentiments
Adam Smith

QTY

This work from 1749. contains original theories of conscience amd moral judgment and it is the foundation for systemof morals.

Philosophy   ISBN: *1-59462-777-0*   Pages:536
MSRP *$19.95*

Jessica's First Prayer
Hesba Stretton

QTY

In a screened and secluded corner of one of the many railway-bridges which span the streets of London there could be seen a few years ago, from five o'clock every morning until half past eight, a tidily set-out coffee-stall, consisting of a trestle and board, upon which stood two large tin cans, with a small fire of charcoal burning under each so as to keep the coffee boiling during the early hours of the morning when the work-people were thronging into the city on their way to their daily toil...

Childrens   ISBN: *1-59462-373-2*   Pages:84
MSRP *$9.95*

My Life and Work
Henry Ford

QTY

Henry Ford revolutionized the world with his implementation of mass production for the Model T automobile. Gain valuable business insight into his life and work with his own auto-biography... "We have only started on our development of our country we have not as yet, with all our talk of wonderful progress, done more than scratch the surface. The progress has been wonderful enough but..."

Biographies/   ISBN: *1-59462-198-5*   Pages:300
MSRP *$21.95*

www.bookjungle.com email: sales@bookjungle.com fax: 630-214-0564 mail: Book Jungle PO Box 2226 Champaign, IL 61825

The Art of Cross-Examination
Francis Wellman

QTY

I presume it is the experience of every author, after his first book is published upon an important subject, to be almost overwhelmed with a wealth of ideas and illustrations which could readily have been included in his book, and which to his own mind, at least, seem to make a second edition inevitable. Such certainly was the case with me; and when the first edition had reached its sixth impression in five months, I rejoiced to learn that it seemed to my publishers that the book had met with a sufficiently favorable reception to justify a second and considerably enlarged edition. ..

Reference   ISBN: *1-59462-647-2*   **Pages:412**
                                      MSRP $19.95

On the Duty of Civil Disobedience
Henry David Thoreau

QTY

Thoreau wrote his famous essay, On the Duty of Civil Disobedience, as a protest against an unjust but popular war and the immoral but popular institution of slave-owning. He did more than write—he declined to pay his taxes, and was hauled off to gaol in consequence. Who can say how much this refusal of his hastened the end of the war and of slavery ?

Law   ISBN: *1-59462-747-9*   **Pages:48**
                                      MSRP $7.45

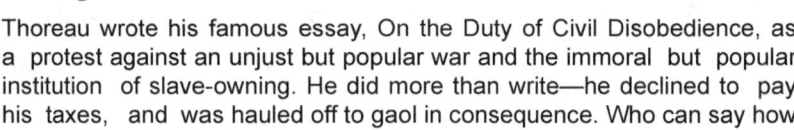

Dream Psychology Psychoanalysis for Beginners
Sigmund Freud

QTY

Sigmund Freud, born Sigismund Schlomo Freud (May 6, 1856 - September 23, 1939), was a Jewish-Austrian neurologist and psychiatrist who co-founded the psychoanalytic school of psychology. Freud is best known for his theories of the unconscious mind, especially involving the mechanism of repression; his redefinition of sexual desire as mobile and directed towards a wide variety of objects; and his therapeutic techniques, especially his understanding of transference in the therapeutic relationship and the presumed value of dreams as sources of insight into unconscious desires.

Psychology   ISBN: *1-59462-905-6*   **Pages:196**
                                      MSRP $15.45

The Miracle of Right Thought
Orison Swett Marden

QTY

Believe with all of your heart that you will do what you were made to do. When the mind has once formed the habit of holding cheerful, happy, prosperous pictures, it will not be easy to form the opposite habit. It does not matter how improbable or how far away this realization may see, or how dark the prospects may be, if we visualize them as best we can, as vividly as possible, hold tenaciously to them and vigorously struggle to attain them, they will gradually become actualized, realized in the life. But a desire, a longing without endeavor, a yearning abandoned or held indifferently will vanish without realization.

Self Help   ISBN: *1-59462-644-8*   **Pages:360**
                                      MSRP $25.45

www.bookjungle.com email: sales@bookjungle.com fax: 630-214-0564 mail: Book Jungle PO Box 2226 Champaign, IL 61825

QTY

	Title	ISBN	Price
☐	**The Rosicrucian Cosmo-Conception Mystic Christianity** by *Max Heindel* *The Rosicrucian Cosmo-conception is not dogmatic, neither does it appeal to any other authority than the reason of the student. It is: not controversial, but is: sent forth in the, hope that it may help to clear...* New Age/Religion Pages 646	1-59462-188-8	$38.95
☐	**Abandonment To Divine Providence** by *Jean-Pierre de Caussade* *"The Rev. Jean Pierre de Caussade was one of the most remarkable spiritual writers of the Society of Jesus in France in the 18th Century. His death took place at Toulouse in 1751. His works have gone through many editions and have been republished...* Inspirational/Religion Pages 400	1-59462-228-0	$25.95
☐	**Mental Chemistry** by *Charles Haanel* *Mental Chemistry allows the change of material conditions by combining and appropriately utilizing the power of the mind. Much like applied chemistry creates something new and unique out of careful combinations of chemicals the mastery of mental chemistry...* New Age Pages 354	1-59462-192-6	$23.95
☐	**The Letters of Robert Browning and Elizabeth Barret Barrett 1845-1846 vol II** by *Robert Browning* and *Elizabeth Barrett* Biographies Pages 596	1-59462-193-4	$35.95
☐	**Gleanings In Genesis (volume I)** by *Arthur W. Pink* *Appropriately has Genesis been termed "the seed plot of the Bible" for in it we have, in germ form, almost all of the great doctrines which are afterwards fully developed in the books of Scripture which follow...* Religion/Inspirational Pages 420	1-59462-130-6	$27.45
☐	**The Master Key** by *L. W. de Laurence* *In no branch of human knowledge has there been a more lively increase of the spirit of research during the past few years than in the study of Psychology, Concentration and Mental Discipline. The requests for authentic lessons in Thought Control, Mental Discipline and...* New Age/Business Pages 422	1-59462-001-6	$30.95
☐	**The Lesser Key Of Solomon Goetia** by *L. W. de Laurence* *This translation of the first book of the "Lernegton" which is now for the first time made accessible to students of Talismanic Magic was done, after careful collation and edition, from numerous Ancient Manuscripts in Hebrew, Latin, and French...* New Age/Occult Pages 92	1-59462-092-X	$9.95
☐	**Rubaiyat Of Omar Khayyam** by *Edward Fitzgerald* *Edward Fitzgerald, whom the world has already learned, in spite of his own efforts to remain within the shadow of anonymity, to look upon as one of the rarest poets of the century, was born at Bredfield, in Suffolk, on the 31st of March, 1809. He was the third son of John Purcell...* Music Pages 172	1-59462-332-5	$13.95
☐	**Ancient Law** by *Henry Maine* *The chief object of the following pages is to indicate some of the earliest ideas of mankind, as they are reflected in Ancient Law, and to point out the relation of those ideas to modern thought.* Religiom/History Pages 452	1-59462-128-4	$29.95
☐	**Far-Away Stories** by *William J. Locke* *"Good wine needs no bush, but a collection of mixed vintages does. And this book is just such a collection. Some of the stories I do not want to remain buried for ever in the museum files of dead magazine-numbers an author's not unpardonable vanity..."* Fiction Pages 272	1-59462-129-2	$19.45
☐	**Life of David Crockett** by *David Crockett* *"Colonel David Crockett was one of the most remarkable men of the times in which he lived. Born in humble life, but gifted with a strong will, an indomitable courage, and unremitting perseverance...* Biographies/New Age Pages 424	1-59462-250-7	$27.45
☐	**Lip-Reading** by *Edward Nitchie* *Edward B. Nitchie, founder of the New York School for the Hard of Hearing, now the Nitchie School of Lip-Reading, Inc, wrote "LIP-READING Principles and Practice". The development and perfecting of this meritorious work on lip-reading was an undertaking...* How-to Pages 400	1-59462-206-X	$25.95
☐	**A Handbook of Suggestive Therapeutics, Applied Hypnotism, Psychic Science** by *Henry Munro* Health/New Age/Health/Self-help Pages 376	1-59462-214-0	$24.95
☐	**A Doll's House: and Two Other Plays** by *Henrik Ibsen* *Henrik Ibsen created this classic when in revolutionary 1848 Rome. Introducing some striking concepts in playwriting for the realist genre, this play has been studied the world over.* Fiction/Classics/Plays 308	1-59462-112-8	$19.95
☐	**The Light of Asia** by *sir Edwin Arnold* *In this poetic masterpiece, Edwin Arnold describes the life and teachings of Buddha. The man who was to become known as Buddha to the world was born as Prince Gautama of India but he rejected the worldly riches and abandoned the reigns of power when...* Religion/History/Biographies Pages 170	1-59462-204-3	$13.95
☐	**The Complete Works of Guy de Maupassant** by *Guy de Maupassant* *"For days and days, nights and nights, I had dreamed of that first kiss which was to consecrate our engagement, and I knew not on what spot I should put my lips..."* Fiction/Classics Pages 240	1-59462-157-8	$16.95
☐	**The Art of Cross-Examination** by *Francis L. Wellman* *Written by a renowned trial lawyer, Wellman imparts his experience and uses case studies to explain how to use psychology to extract desired information through questioning.* How-to/Science/Reference Pages 408	1-59462-309-0	$26.95
☐	**Answered or Unanswered?** by *Louisa Vaughan* *Miracles of Faith in China* Religion Pages 112	1-59462-248-5	$10.95
☐	**The Edinburgh Lectures on Mental Science (1909)** by *Thomas* *This book contains the substance of a course of lectures recently given by the writer in the Queen Street Hall, Edinburgh. Its purpose is to indicate the Natural Principles governing the relation between Mental Action and Material Conditions...* New Age/Psychology Pages 148	1-59462-008-3	$11.95
☐	**Ayesha** by *H. Rider Haggard* *Verily and indeed it is the unexpected that happens! Probably if there was one person upon the earth from whom the Editor of this, and of a certain previous history, did not expect to hear again...* Classics Pages 380	1-59462-301-5	$24.95
☐	**Ayala's Angel** by *Anthony Trollope* *The two girls were both pretty, but Lucy who was twenty-one who supposed to be simple and comparatively unattractive, whereas Ayala was credited, as her Bombwhat romantic name might show, with poetic charm and a taste for romance. Ayala when her father died was nineteen...* Fiction Pages 484	1-59462-352-X	$29.95
☐	**The American Commonwealth** by *James Bryce* *An interpretation of American democratic political theory. It examines political mechanics and society from the perspective of Scotsman James Bryce* Politics Pages 572	1-59462-286-8	$34.45
☐	**Stories of the Pilgrims** by *Margaret P. Pumphrey* *This book explores pilgrims religious oppression in England as well as their escape to Holland and eventual crossing to America on the Mayflower, and their early days in New England...* History Pages 268	1-59462-116-0	$17.95

www.bookjungle.com *email:* sales@bookjungle.com *fax:* 630-214-0564 *mail:* Book Jungle PO Box 2226 Champaign, IL 61825

QTY

The Fasting Cure *by Sinclair Upton* ISBN: *1-59462-222-1* **$13.95**
In the Cosmopolitan Magazine for May, 1910, and in the Contemporary Review (London) for April, 1910, I published an article dealing with my experiences in fasting. I have written a great many magazine articles, but never one which attracted so much attention... New Age/Self Help/Health Pages 164

Hebrew Astrology *by Sepharial* ISBN: *1-59462-308-2* **$13.45**
In these days of advanced thinking it is a matter of common observation that we have left many of the old landmarks behind and that we are now pressing forward to greater heights and to a wider horizon than that which represented the mind-content of our progenitors... Astrology Pages 144

Thought Vibration or The Law of Attraction in the Thought World ISBN: *1-59462-127-6* **$12.95**
by William Walker Atkinson Psychology/Religion Pages 144

Optimism *by Helen Keller* ISBN: *1-59462-108-X* **$15.95**
Helen Keller was blind, deaf, and mute since 19 months old, yet famously learned how to overcome these handicaps, communicate with the world, and spread her lectures promoting optimism. An inspiring read for everyone... Biographies/Inspirational Pages 84

Sara Crewe *by Frances Burnett* ISBN: *1-59462-360-0* **$9.45**
In the first place, Miss Minchin lived in London. Her home was a large, dull, tall one, in a large, dull square, where all the houses were alike, and all the sparrows were alike, and where all the door-knockers made the same heavy sound... Childrens/Classic Pages 88

The Autobiography of Benjamin Franklin *by Benjamin Franklin* ISBN: *1-59462-135-7* **$24.95**
The Autobiography of Benjamin Franklin has probably been more extensively read than any other American historical work, and no other book of its kind has had such ups and downs of fortune. Franklin lived for many years in England, where he was agent... Biographies/History Pages 332

Name	
Email	
Telephone	
Address	
City, State ZIP	

☐ Credit Card   ☐ Check / Money Order

Credit Card Number	
Expiration Date	
Signature	

Please Mail to: Book Jungle
PO Box 2226
Champaign, IL 61825
or Fax to: 630-214-0564

ORDERING INFORMATION
web: *www.bookjungle.com*
email: *sales@bookjungle.com*
fax: *630-214-0564*
mail: *Book Jungle PO Box 2226 Champaign, IL 61825*
or PayPal *to sales@bookjungle.com*

Please contact us for bulk discounts

DIRECT-ORDER TERMS

**20% Discount if You Order
Two or More Books**
Free Domestic Shipping!
Accepted: Master Card, Visa,
Discover, American Express

11.621　4367lCB000l5B/2686　[210119811]